CONTEMPORARY WRITERS

General Editors
MALCOLM BRADBURY
and
CHRISTOPHER BIGSBY

JOHN FOWLES

JOHN
FOWLES

PETER CONRADI

METHUEN
LONDON AND NEW YORK

First published in 1982 by
Methuen & Co. Ltd
11 New Fetter Lane, London EC4P 4EE
Reprinted 1983
Published in the USA by
Methuen & Co.
in association with Methuen, Inc.
733 Third Avenue, New York, NY 10017

Typeset by Rowland Phototypesetting Ltd
Printed in Great Britain by
Richard Clay (The Chaucer Press) Ltd
Bungay, Suffolk

British Library Cataloguing in Publication Data

Conradi, Peter
John Fowles. – (Contemporary writers)
1. Fowles, John – Criticism and interpretation
I. Title   II. Series
823'.914   PR6056.085
ISBN 0-416-32250-6

Library of Congress Cataloging in Publication Data

Conradi, Peter, 1932–
John Fowles.
(Contemporary writers)
Bibliography: p.
1. Fowles, John – Criticism and interpretation.
I. Title.   II. Series.
PR6056.085Z63   1982   823'.914   81-22572
ISBN 0-416-32250-6 (pbk.)   AACR2

In memoriam
Florence Alice Conradi
née Josephi 1892–1983

CONTENTS

GENERAL EDITORS' PREFACE

The contemporary is a country which we all inhabit, but there is little agreement as to its boundaries or its shape. The serious writer is one of its most sensitive interpreters, but criticism is notoriously cautious in offering a response or making a judgement. Accordingly, this continuing series is an endeavour to look at some of the most important writers of our time, and the questions raised by their work. It is, in effect, an attempt to map the contemporary, to describe its aesthetic and moral topography.

The series came into existence out of two convictions. One was that, despite all the modern pressures on the writer and on literary culture, we live in a major creative time, as vigorous and alive in its distinctive way as any that went before. The other was that, though criticism itself tends to grow more theoretical and apparently indifferent to contemporary creation, there are grounds for a lively aesthetic debate. This series, which includes books written from various standpoints, is meant to provide a forum for that debate. By design, some of those who have contributed are themselves writers, willing to respond to their contemporaries; others are critics who have brought to the discussion of current writing the spirit of contemporary criticism or simply a conviction, forcibly and coherently argued, for the contemporary significance of their subjects. Our aim, as the series develops, is to continue to explore the works of major post-war writers – in fiction, drama

9

and poetry – over an international range, and thereby to illuminate not only those works but also in some degree the artistic, social and moral assumptions on which they rest. Our wish is that, in their very variety of approach and emphasis, these books will stimulate interest in and understanding of the vitality of a living literature which, because it is contemporary, is especially ours.

Norwich, England   MALCOLM BRADBURY
                                        CHRISTOPHER BIGSBY

ACKNOWLEDGEMENTS

I should like to thank John Fowles and the University of East Anglia for permission to quote from a UEA interview, and the editors of *Critical Quarterly* for permission to use material which first appeared in that journal.

In writing this book, I owe much to discussions with Dr Vic Sage, Professor Malcolm Bradbury and the members of his graduate seminar on post-modernism, and the members of a seminar of my own on twentieth-century fiction, all at the University of East Anglia. Simon Edwards, Dr P. Martin and Jim O'Neill read parts of the book and commented helpfully. Terri Gomez helped by transcribing material; Martin Corner scrutinized the typescript and made many useful suggestions; so did Daphne Turner; and Simon Loveday gave generous assistance with secondary sources. The faults of the book remain, of course, my own.

Kingston Polytechnic, 1982   PETER CONRADI

A NOTE ON THE TEXTS

Page references for quotations from John Fowles's fiction are to the English paperback editions. The following abbreviations have been used. For full details see the Bibliography.

Works by John Fowles:

C	*The Collector*
A	*The Aristos*
M	*The Magus*
FLW	*The French Lieutenant's Woman*
ET	*The Ebony Tower*
DM	*Daniel Martin*
MR	*The Magus: A Revised Version*
'Notes'	'Notes on a Unfinished Novel' (in *NT*)
'Hardy'	'Hardy and the Hag'
'I Write'	'I Write Therefore I Am'
'On Being English'	'On Being English but not British'

Interviews:

B	Richard Boston, 'John Fowles, Alone But Not Lonely', *New York Times Book Review*, 9 November 1969, pp. 2, 52–3
BBC	'Desert Island Discs', BBC Radio, January 1981 (unpublished)
C	J. Campbell, 'An Interview with John Fowles', *Contemporary Literature*, 17, 4 (1976), pp. 455–69

H	Daniel Halpern, 'A Sort of Exile in Lyme Regis', *London Magazine*, 10 (March 1971), pp. 34–46
N	Roy Newquist, 'John Fowles', *Counterpoint* (Chicago, Ill.: Rand McNally, 1964), pp. 217–25
R	Robert Robinson, 'Giving the Reader a Choice – a Conversation with John Fowles', *The Listener*, 31 October 1974, p. 584
S	Lorna Sage, 'Profile 7: John Fowles', *New Review* (1974)
UEA	University of East Anglia interviews, 1976 (unpublished)
ZB	Heide Ziegler and Christopher Bigsby (eds), *The Radical Imagination and the Liberal Tradition: Interviews with Contemporary English and American Novelists* (London: Junction Books, 1982)

Other publications:

JML	*Journal of Modern Literature*, 8, 2 (1980–1), John Fowles Special Number
NT	Malcolm Bradbury (ed.), *The Novel Today* (Manchester and London: Manchester University Press and Fontana, 1977)

1

JOHN FOWLES AND THE MODERN ROMANCE

. . . to be oneself is the aim of every romantic. (W. H. Auden, *The Enchafed Flood*)

John Fowles's achievement has proved a hard one to assess, and not merely in the way that all contemporary writing is properly resistant to a just critical focus. He is an immensely popular writer, one of whose novels, *The French Lieutenant's Woman*, rapidly became a set text in universities. He possesses a seductive narrative drive which would be the envy of any Victorian serial novelist. He once wrote a novel in eighteen days and wrote the first drafts for *The Collector* and *The Ebony Tower* in one month each (H, p. 40). There are reports of ten unpublished novels. His fictions display anxieties about being serious as well as about being entertaining, and his flamboyantly showy fluency is itself a value he clearly suspects; the novels worry at it in the attempt to solicit a series of impossible liberations. In *The Collector* a beautiful kidnapped girl struggles to free herself from her deranged captor. In *The Magus* the struggle is against the authorial surrogate Conchis, whose totalitarian yet benign fantasy is paradoxically to educate the protagonist into a properly difficult sense of his own freedom. In *The French Lieutenant's Woman*, his most important work so far, it is the emancipation of the reader as well as the major characters from the coercions of the text which is part of the programme. Imprisonment and liberation, seduction and betrayal, are both thematic and formal obsessions for Fowles. He makes adroit use of the collaborative privileges of verbal form, soliciting the reader in fiction's felt need to authenticate itself (capturing/seducing the reader) and in its equal, contrary need to expose its own tricksterism, the artifice upon which any such authentication must ultimately rest (betraying/liberating the reader).

Fowles writes romances, gothic stories that exploit the ancient erotic sources and opportunities of narrative and whose designs on the reader are palpable; and through which a series of Persecuted Maidens and *princesses lointaines* are pursued and prompted, like the mystical and psychological truths they embody, to deny the text that closure they seek. In the magical enclosures in which his fictions abound, love is feudalized. He is a paradoxical figure: a didactic and coercive libertarian; an evolutionary socialist profoundly committed to the values of a Romantic individualism, which his existentialism is called upon to validate; an apologist for the female-principle much given to imagining the sexual exploitation and salvation of women; a writer of fables of erotic quest who does not present adult sexual relations, and who has been read as a bourgeois pornographer expert in the aesthetics of frustration – but which expertise is itself put at the service of a censorious sexual moralism.

Fowles has an evident willingness to risk himself in each of his fictions in something new, so that each novel can also be read as an innovatory attack on his own fluency. What each fiction also shares is a curiosity about the technical and ethical potentialities of what have traditionally been regarded as 'low' sub-genres of fiction, all of them broadly categories of romance. Romance seeks what Hawthorne termed 'the truth of the human heart', often through a conscious simplification and allegorizing of character. Its mythic tableaux try to reimport the marvellous and improbable back into human life: it 're-makes the world in the image of desire' and imagines ideal and idiosyncratic worlds. Both *The Magus* and 'The Ebony Tower' differently approach romance in its pure state; 'Poor Koko' and *The Collector* utilize the thriller, *The French Lieutenant's Woman* the historical romance and sensation novel, and 'The Enigma' the detective tale. In each, the interest of the fiction lies in the consequences of disconfirming the expectations raised by the genre. 'Then if our story disobeys the unreal literary rules, that might mean it's actually truer to life?' as Isabel asks in 'The Enigma' (*ET*, p. 236).

The romance, it is worth recalling, has traditionally been regarded with more suspicion in England than in America, and has been liable to derogation as a mode of lowbrow entertainment, of sentimental and fantastic escape. Coleridge's fierce dismissal of Scott's novels as 'Wretched trash', as Ronald Binns points out, has set the tone.[1] British criticism at its least generous has tended to blame Fowles's novels simultaneously for stooping and aspiring, treating them – like the Hollywood fantasies excoriated in *Daniel Martin* – as both ruthlessly sensationalist in their manipulation of expectation and relentlessly high-minded in their moral tenor. The four books or monographs so far published on Fowles have all been American.[2] The American critic Robert Scholes suggests that it is a 'fair and important question' whether Fowles's passion in *The Magus* is 'equal to his virtuosity, whether the book is merely sensational or truly meaningful'.[3] Through moralizing his romances so insistently, however – 'I teach better if I seduce' (S, p. 35) is how he has put it – Fowles has made himself vulnerable to attack both from those critics whose aesthetic puritanism finds his ethically controlled fantasies didactic, and from those whose humanist puritanism finds them escapist. From some of those critics characterized by Paul de Man as content to be communal moralists in the morning and formalists in the afternoon,[4] and from a vast non-academic audience, he has had a responsive reading.

Romance was described by Henry James as '*experience liberated* so to speak; experience disengaged, disembroiled, disencumbered, exempt from the conditions we usually know how to attach to it' (my italics), such a disconnection working most intensely, James suggests, when 'the sacrifice of community, of the "related" sides of situations, has not been too rash'.[5] The spatialization of the relations between romance and realism, which James goes on to develop, is a mode of vision

17

natural to Fowles too: romance is conceived of as a mode of levitation. 'The omnipotent power of gravity in the novel form is realism. I resist it less and less' (ZB, p. 123). All his novels differently marry literary modes and embattle styles. What distinguishes *The Magus* (1965) and *The French Lieutenant's Woman* (1969) is the way the conventions of realism and romance are made in the first to cohabit uneasily, in the second to collide openly. In *The Magus* Urfe's extraordinary adventures on a remote Greek island are subject by him to a constant, impossible series of attempts to authenticate them, to verify their basis; in *The French Lieutenant's Woman* the reader is wryly invited from the first page to test out the 'truths' of the narration, an invitation the novel extends in a variety of ways. As Binns argues, 'Fowles inverts the traditionally assumed dichotomy between the romancer and the realist writer, manipulating the romance form to effect a sceptical examination of the romance experience and, more radically, a critique of contemporary realist fiction for its lack of moral responsibility.'[6]

But Fowles is, as I shall argue, himself a romantic artist as well as a writer utilizing the romance tradition, and for romantic artists, as W. H. Auden wittily put it, 'the Boojum [is] waiting at the next cross-roads where they will be asked whether or not they have become their actual selves.'[7] The Fowlesian novel is always a new quest for personal authenticity, a place in which the self of the protagonist is to be tested, tried, stripped and subjected to ordeal. In his best books this testing is formal as well as thematic. In *The Magus* and *The French Lieutenant's Woman* Urfe and Smithson search for authenticity and are consequently denounced, in books that equally denounce themselves and try to purge their own inauthenticities by publicizing them. The development of the novel is frequently now mythographically presented as in Hegelian evolution towards a place of full self-consciousness, where the 'bad faith' or lack of innocence involved in the necessary conventionalization of *all* art eventually become thematized. The moment in which the work offers a pleasurable rebuke to the reader's credulity ('Fuck all this lying' is a notorious *topos* from B. S. Johnson's *Albert Angelo* (1964)) has itself become a new convention; contemporary fiction has been subject to a Platonic guilt about its ontological status, which in turn has led to a puritan refusal of, or a witty exultation in, the wicked consolations and equivocations of form. 'Novels are lies, novelists disreputable people in their basic natures,' argues Angus Wilson.[8] 'I know that nothing consoles and nothing justifies except a story – but that doesn't stop all stories from being lies,' asserted a character from Iris Murdoch's *Under the Net* (1954), in a philosophic dialogue that is itself fraudulent.

Such a 'progress' must be a paradoxical one. The formal self-consciousness of much contemporary literature can also be read as the development of individualism to a point feared if advocated by nineteenth-century liberalism – as Sheldon Rothblatt, writing about *The French Lieutenant's Woman*, has argued. The search for an absolute existential wholeness can never be fully achieved by either work or hero. Even the work that gleefully announces itself as a garden of forking paths, as *The French Lieutenant's Woman* tries to, is still a reticent accomplice of the world's bad conscience: that novel awards us and its characters three possible endings and proclaims our liberation and that of the protagonists to be a settled matter. (Life, as Christopher Ricks pointed out, would give us not three possibilities but an infinity of them.) If to be oneself is the aim of everything romantic, it is not an aim that can ever be wholly achieved. And indeed Fowles has acknowledged this: 'But *The French Lieutenant's Woman* was a cheat, you see. I thought it was an obvious cheat' (S, p. 35). Total self-coincidence always lies in the future – for the work and its agents as for the reader – or in the past where, in one necessary map of misreading, the Victorian novel can be pastoralized as a place Edenically unaware of its own conventionalization, awaiting like Milton's Adam that *felix culpa* of a Fall into Modernity which will enable it to start to know itself. The cloud of formal unknowing in which the nineteenth-century realist novel innocently and sinfully moves is itself a part of the subject-matter of *The French Lieutenant's Woman*. That mutual criticism of realism and romance which in *The Magus* made for an uncomfortable liaison reappears in *The French Lieutenant's Woman* as a more controlled formal irony. This novel, like certain mannerist art, puts its own conventions on a kind of show trial, convicting itself in public of deception, but oddly intensifying its own illusionism in so doing. The show trial turns out to be (like that of Urfe in *The Magus*, and like those of the 1930s) itself a kind of *trompe-l'œil*.

Closure, illusionism and a hierarchy of discourse figure in a recent critical work as the defining characteristics of classic realism, that purportedly inauthentic mode.[9] Fowles's novels show disturbances in all three areas. The hierarchy of discourse – which asserts the subordination of most levels in favour of one privileged level of discourse whose hegemony is finally asserted (closure) – is challenged in *The French Lieutenant's Woman*, where two endings are granted near equality: the expectation of a simple closure is frustrated. In *The Magus* the denial of closure is accompanied by an equivocation about whether the illusionism of the opening section, or the very different style of illusionism asserted at Bourani, will win the implied competition between them; neither level wholly agrees to accept subordinate status. Even *The Collector*, which apart from *Daniel Martin* shows the greatest debt to realism, has a penultimate chapter in which Clegg offers his ideal ending, an ending invalidated by the real last chapter. And this real ending in its turn is undercut by Clegg's plan to kidnap a new victim and re-establish the cycle of imprisonment. The open ending of *The Magus* and of some of the short stories, and the trick endings of *The French Lieutenant's Woman*, are also all part of 'a sort of theory that the energy is in the ill-defined' (R), an attempt to imprison contingency or institutionalize provisionality. This same dedication to the provisional led Fowles to recall the text of *The Magus* and issue a revised version in 1977.

The formal unselfconsciousness of realism makes it, we have been taught to believe, a mode of low credulity leading to ideological entrapment. It is a form of collaboration with the epistemological and political status quo, faking up the pastoral vision of a stable and publicly knowable world containing unique moral agents; it is just such a status quo that the higher scepticism of the fictionalist or fabulating freedom-fighter (in the most recent and challenging version of fictive disconnection) bravely subverts by opposing a more accurate, and festive, indeterminacy. The tension between these two views – between satisfying our credulity and appeasing our scepticism, as David Lodge has it – differently energizes each of Fowles's first three novels. When as in *Daniel Martin* such tensions are relaxed, the result is an unhappily indulgent and incontinent solipsism, the more singular in that it is apparently unwitting.

From a different angle, as Lodge has argued, realism itself can usefully be seen as an ancestrally impure and precarious synthesis of history, romance and allegory; and from this point of view it is the problematizing of the relations between its constituent parts which characterizes much contemporary British fiction, including Fowles's. Problematic fiction in this sense might be typified by Doris Lessing's *The Golden Notebook* (1962), by Angus Wilson's *No Laughing Matter* (1967) and, albeit differently, by Iris Murdoch's *The Black Prince* (1973), as well as by *The French Lieutenant's Woman* – works whose formal aporia and hesitation coexist with immense formal energy and inventiveness. These novels might be said to carry the currently inescapable and romantic rhetoric of *insubordination* (subversion and undercutting, transgression and destabilization) circumspectly, as if wittily aware of their paradoxical dependence on the existence of fatherly host-conventions without which neither parasites nor parricides could subsist. They leave the reader, as Lodge has suggested, with a paradox about the relations between art and life:

The reality principle is never allowed to lapse entirely – indeed, it is often invoked . . . to expose the artificiality of conventional realistic illusion. . . . The kind of novelist I am talking about retains a loyalty to both ['reality' *and* fiction], but lacks the orthodox novelist's confidence in the possibility of reconciling them. He makes the difficulty of the task, in a sense, his subject. (*NT*, p. 105)

In a period in which the debate about the degree of integrity available to either the 'self' or the 'text' is an urgent cultural issue as well as a literary-critical battleground, it is not surprising that Fowles's work, impenitently hybrid as it is, should have received such diverse readings. Each of his novels can best be read as in pursuit of the peculiar integrity of its own incompleteness, which is to say as braving a new kind of fictional logic by which to foreground, however inconclusively, its necessary inauthenticities.

*

Fowles was born in 1926 in Leigh-on-Sea in Essex; he found it respectable, conformist and suburban. Later he wrote that 'The rows of respectable little houses inhabited by respectable little people had an early depressive effect on me and I believe that they caused my intense and continuing dislike of mankind *en masse*.'[10] His attachment to that liberal individualism, which such a middle-class environment might be seen to encourage as well as to frustrate, is apparent throughout his work. During the war his family evacuated to a small Devonshire village near Dartmoor – an experience he drew on for the first chapter of *Daniel Martin*. Its description there prefigures a later chapter, 'The Sacred Combe', in which he discusses the literary tradition of an opposing pastoral world in which the self can magically transcend the contradictions in its relations with society. He borrows the term 'La Bonne Vaux' from Restif de la Bretonne as a figure for this necessary inner artistic retreat. His fiction deals in both these types of enclosure, the prison-house of restrictive convention and the green playground for the self: the cellar or crypt in its lost garden in *The Collector* in which Miranda is imprisoned; the Alain-Fournier-like lost domains of *The Magus* and 'The Ebony Tower' in which Urfe and Williams find and lose themselves. The mid-nineteenth century itself in *The French Lieutenant's Woman* appears as the most impressive of these magical uterine enclosures, a prison of repressive censorship which simultaneously contains the lush paradise Ware Commons, a zone of scandalously joyous taxonomic and moral indiscipline. Such landscapes belong, of course, to the basic grammar of the Romantic Revival, places 'freed from the evils and responsibilities of communal life, in which the exceptional individual encounters either the drought of a more extreme alienation and longing or an ideal nourishment. The image of the happy Pre-Lapsarian Place appears often enough in Romantic literature but charged usually with a hopeless nostalgia. The examples which the romantic actually encounters turn out to be mirages or disappointing and dangerous deserts.'[11] The subterranean connection between the two kinds of landscape – between drought and fertility – is evident in *The Magus*, where Bourani is a place of illusion to which Urfe is driven to acquire disillusion, a place in which pain and pleasure come close; and in *The Collector*, where it is Miranda's imprisonment that begins to emancipate her. In an early essay ('On Being English But Not British') Fowles draws on the romantic image of Robin Hood to sanction the idea of England itself as just such a potentially 'green' world, and to suggest that the English talent for duplicitous politeness enables the survival there of the substantial self: under cover of civility the English outlaw their essential beings to a place of happy exile, in which an ideal justice for ever underwrites liberal individualism. Robin Hood figures again both in *The Aristos* and *Daniel Martin*.

Fowles was sent to Bedford School, an English public school where he became head boy:

> Being head boy was a weird experience. You had total power over 800 other boys, you were totally responsible for discipline and punishment. . . . I suppose I used to beat on average three or four boys a day. . . . Very evil, I think. Terrible system. (B)

After a spell near the end of the war in the Marines, he went to Oxford, where he read French and German. He then spent some dozen years teaching in various positions, as *lecteur* in

English at the University of Poitiers in France, at the Anargyrios College on the island of Spetsai in Greece (an environment he drew on for the background of *The Magus*), and then in two colleges in and around London. The publication of *The Collector* and its rapid success in 1963 enabled him to give up teaching.

It might be said that the ambivalence towards the authority of the text that Fowles's work evinces is reflected in various ways by the history of his own relationship to power, and by the manner in which 'form' in his own life has appeared as temptation and consolation. When in an interview he speaks of his belief in the 'character-building novel' (S, p. 32), it is hard to forget how indebted the phrase is to the rhetoric of the English public school; or, for that matter, how didactically his novels similarly challenge the reader at their close to 'stand on their own two feet'. Just as he sees himself as a reformed practitioner of the pleasures of petty school power, so he has also described himself as a reformed collector, hunter and, in a sense, gardener: having enjoyed hunting and killing as a boy, he now collects nothing more sinister than, for example, seventeenth-century theology, old plays, postcards of Edwardian actresses, and spiders which he drowns in tequila. He is married and lives near the sea in Lyme Regis, a setting he used (before moving there) in *The French Lieutenant's Woman*. A part of his garden is left to itself, freed, as it were, from the plot of the gardener, and it gives him special pleasure and instruction. Naturalism, partly informed by attitudes learnt from Zen, is an important part of Fowles's life and books (he has written on *Islands* and *The Tree*) and affects his attitude to people: 'there is nothing nicer to me than sitting in a window over a street and just watching how these weird bipeds pass each other and speak to each other' (UEA). His range of reading includes Sartre, Camus, Alain-Fournier, Peacock and Hardy, by all of whom he has been influenced in some way, and, in a random list, twelfth-century romance, Defoe, D. H. Lawrence, Montaigne, Flaubert, John Berryman. In the novels an equally generous narrative enthusiasm and a recoil from determining authority coexist with the compulsion to explore coercive and manipulative narrative power.

Both are apparent in Fowles's collection of philosophical apophthegms *The Aristos*, originally subtitled 'A Self-Portrait in Ideas'. This book has been a problem for his admirers, and he has said 'I hate to think of the awful pages of bad philosophy that would be in my novels if I hadn't written that. I regard it a little as a dustbin' (UEA). He none the less revised and reissued the book in 1968 with a preface, and it combines plain good sense with mystagogy – arguing for, among other things, zero population growth and universal education, and against nationalism – and magisterially expounding noscentrism, the Nemo and the relativity of recompense on the way. It is written in what it terms 'the form of notes . . . in an attempt to suppress all rhetoric, all persuasion through style . . . to banish all possibility of persuasion through artificial means' (p. 13). A few pages later it reminds the reader 'You may die before turning the next page' (p. 18). The desire to exercise histrionically coercive narrative gifts yet find an escape from the responsibility of doing so – to marry dogma and provisionality – are each quintessentially Fowlesian; but he can manage his own mock-modest disappearances and abscondings better in the novels. *The Aristos* is pulled at by the values of an evolutionary socialism as well as by those of a romantic bourgeois individualism, and it employs existentialism to solemnize their liaison. In this sub-Nietzschean 'Thus Spake John Fowles' the casual afflatus is in fact deeply rehearsed, and its immodest straining after the lapidary precludes its arriving at much original or fastidious thought.[12]

One importance of *The Aristos* for Fowles's readers lies, however, in the light it throws on the debt his liberalism owes to existentialism.[13] Fowles belongs to that generation typified by E. P. Thompson as opting, in reaction against the ideological extremism of the mid-century, for the absolute of personal integrity.[14] The quest for such an absolute clearly attracted Fowles to the new existentialist wisdom and the intellectual climate of France under the Fourth Republic. *The Aristos*, having spoken of fascism as being 'at its Platonic best the most realistic of political philosophies', goes on to oppose to it existentialism, which for Fowles enshrines 'this obstinate individualism' that makes for 'the revolt of the individual against all those systems of thought . . . that attempt to rob him of his individuality' (p. 122). The chief concern of *The Aristos* was 'to preserve the freedom of the individual against all those pressures to conform that threaten our century' (p. 7). This freedom is dramatically pictured by Fowles as always *in extremis*. 'I want no more specific *prison* than that I express myself in printed words,' he writes, trying to eschew 'the *cage* called novelist' (p. 7; my italics). It is the writer, moreover, who best exemplifies this freedom in adversity. In an early piece, Fowles suggested that the concept of the Few, to which both *The Collector* and *The Aristos* refer, applies pre-eminently to creators ('I Write', p. 90). As for the novels themselves, 'Most of my major characters have been involved in this Sartrean concept of authenticity and inauthenticity' and 'This is the sort of existentialist thesis of the books – that one has to discover one's own feelings' (C, pp. 465–6). In another interview heralding more and more existentialist novels, Fowles suggested that

> One is inauthentic largely because of the pressures of modern society. . . . This giving of a solution is the wonderful thing about existentialism and why I believe it will take the place of the old, dogmatic religions. It allows you to face reality and act creatively in terms of your own powers and your own situation. It's the great individualist philosophy, the twentieth century individual's answer to the evil pressures of both capitalism and communism. (N, p. 225)

Words from the existentialist credo such as 'freedom', 'choice', 'will' and 'hazard' always carry a special charge for Fowles; and the attempt to induct his heroes into 'good faith' takes place against a view of the divisions within mankind that *The Aristos* elucidates. An important section deals with Heraclitus' division of mankind into the Few and the Many, the Aristoi (or good ones) and Hoi Polloi, and then speaks of the extent to which biology underwrites this distinction. In most fields of human endeavour great steps forward are due to 'extraordinary individuals', and the mass of mankind are not highly moral or aesthetically gifted. Most of human history is a struggle between these two groups, and 'My purpose in *The Collector* was to analyse, through a parable, some of the results of this confrontation.' The conflict is exacerbated by, on the one hand, unnecessary envy and, on the other, unnecessary contempt, an understanding of which attenuates its brutality. This is arguably an implicitly Fabian view – that a tutored and responsible élite must urgently humanize and redeem a majority, must assuage the guilt of irremediable privilege and help equalize the rewards – but also an implicitly Platonic view in so far as the soul is envisaged, as in the *Phaedrus*, as an inequitable constituency. The Few are the existentially elect, best represented by creators; and Fowles metamorphoses Heraclitus, Socrates, Pascal and, elsewhere, Jane Austen into proto-existentialists.

The degree to which Fowles has adopted a Romantic and redemptive view of the function of art and the artist should not be underestimated. Fowles's existentialism has never tempted him towards the inverted pathetic fallacy of the French *nouveau roman*. Writers are conceived of as living necessarily in exile, outsiders[15] even in their own country, like Fowles himself (H, *passim*); they are conceived of as potentially heroic super-individuals (*A*, p. 201), self-determining specialists in the mysteries of freedom and choice (N, p. 225); indeed, Fowles has repeatedly stated his belief in inspiration and in those Muses who govern its movements, is a 'total believer in the organic growth of his plots' (*JML*, p. 188), and conceives his novels in a classically Blakean opposition as 'plants' rather than the 'clocks' of mechanistic critical analysis (*JML*, p. 193). He has referred to himself as a 'novelist of loss' (UEA) and pictures the self in Hegelian opposition to the world: 'The age is out to exterminate both the individual and the enduring' ('Notes', p. 144); the eponymous hero of *Daniel Martin* perceives himself as 'excluded, castrated by both capitalism and communism, forbidden to belong' (*DM*, p. 615). The notion of the self and the text as wounded totalities, as potentially absolute self-determining individuals, is, of course, Romantic.

Authenticate, author, authority: his novels seek out some odd aspects of the common derivation of these terms. The converse of the Fowlesian panic at that which threatens to neuter the authentic life-force, is the necessary transcendence of the self – and the text – as forgeries. Thus, in *The Magus*, the exemplary art-works at Bourani turn out to be forgeries, and Urfe himself moves away from inauthenticity towards forging for himself, in both senses, an identity less unoriginal. Even that ellipsis of the subject in a subsidiary clause, which constitutes one of Fowles's most habitual stylistic mannerisms – 'These two were rising in the world; and knew it' (*FLW*, p. 363); 'He did not really live in the manoir; but in the forest outside' (*ET*, p. 82); 'Perhaps she had rehearsed saying this; but still meant it' (*M*, p. 567) – points perhaps to a mystical presence of the subjectivity portentously defying its grammatical absence, an after-image which, in small, mimics that famous extensibility of character beyond its enabling action for which realism itself is famous.

Iris Murdoch is a near contemporary of Fowles, a novelist-philosopher also influenced by existentialism, which, however, she rejected early. The terms of her suspicion of both existentialism and romance illuminate Fowles's work and reception as well as her own. Existentialism is for her one of those dominant philosophies through which an age is pictured.

'It is . . . a natural mode of being of the capitalist era. It is attractive, and indeed to most of us still natural, because it suggests individualism, self-reliance, private conscience, and what we ordinarily think of as political freedom, in that important sense where freedom means not doing what is right but doing what is desired. The beginnings of capitalism and the age of science both produced and needed free-moving independent people.[16]

28

For Murdoch the ills of existentialism are those also of its Romantic Hegelian and Kantian inheritance. It leaves moral philosophy undefended against 'an irresponsible and un-directed self-assertion which goes easily hand in hand with some brand of pseudo-scientific determinism. *An unexamined sense of the strength of the machine is combined with the illusion of jumping out of it*' (my italics).[17] The literature thus produced might be exemplified by Fowles's ingenious story 'The Enigma', in which the most publicly determined of all Fowles's characters, John Marcus Fielding, defies both social and literary convention by jumping out of the plot itself; 'if the man were entirely free he might simply walk out of the story,' Frank Kermode prophesied in a discussion of such freedoms.[18] It is also a literature in which personal conflicts are externalized in tightly contained myths which in turn, and under a guise of emancipation, conceal an adoration of necessity: a literature, as it were, of the liberating enclosure.

Murdoch's view – while it proposes the demotion of Dos-toevsky, Hawthorne and Emily Brontë to a greatness of the second order – none the less involves a recognition that, in our time, the best novels have indeed been metaphysical in just the sense she warns us of, and complicit with a purging away of contingency within themselves.[19] She herself has found it not-ably hard to write according to her own prescriptions. Both Murdoch and Fowles have an extraordinary narrative drive which they differently suspect. Both are atheistic humanists who would wish to find in the contemporary novel a way of rescuing the contingent moral agent from the myth that neces-sarily constitutes that agent. Both are given, in the service of such an emancipation, to exploration of the romance as a genre in which their sense of the mysterious otherness of existence and of its deep psychic responsibilities leads to a dedication to baroque and fantastical effects, to an equivocation about the supernatural, to picturing psychopomps and magi, those adept reality trainers who tutor their circumambient novices into suprarational mystery. Both often picture learning in voyeurist or sado-masochistic terms, see literature as a battle against the bewitchment of the intelligence, and create novels liable to the charge of colluding with the bewitchment they lament. Both, in other words, are precariously involved in a ludic balancing-act in which myth and romance on the one hand and character and historical contingency on the other present opposing temptations. It is noteworthy that Murdoch, a more fastidious intelligence than Fowles, has, despite her attacks on our Romantic inheritance, created gothic romances given to a recurrent eschatological urgency, three of which centre around Persecuted Maidens locked up in Remote Enclosures (*The Unicorn*, 1963; *The Time of the Angels*, 1966; *The Sea, The Sea*, 1978). The attempts to rescue the Maiden, and indeed to unlock an appropriately contemporary 'realism' from the Castle Perilous of romance – to regain a guiltless pre-lapsarian resting-place for the novel's conventions – are unending.

If, for the Fowles reader, the emphasis none the less falls differently, this may be for a number of related reasons. Fowles has recently said: 'I now think of existentialism as a kind of literary metaphor, a wish-fulfilment. I long ago began to doubt whether it had any true philosophical value in its assertions about freedom' (ZB, p. 117). The novel that has so far come out of this retreat, *Daniel Martin*, which attacks his own generation for being '100 per cent selfish' (UEA), is his weakest so far. Moreover, its retreat from existentialism, with its doctrine of conflating selfishness and grace ('mystic voluntarism'; *JML*, p. 207), is by no means complete. It is his fierce commitment to the authentication of his characters and readers that has led to Fowles's attacks on the authority of his texts. Murdoch would regard such a commitment as a part of that destructive Romantic legacy which her *comic* and *other-centred* fictions struggle to attenuate. Fowles's desire to liberate the heroic primacy of the self, by constructing an action that will educate his protagonist but not decentre him, could, on the other hand, be said to be radical in the sense that it involves a return to roots. And this in turn has lent his avant-gardism a curiously old-fashioned flavour. His emphasis on the destiny of the (male) consciousness, with its awe at anything that encloses the agent and threatens his supremacy as a centre of significance, has consequences for the sexual politics of his work – and also for its phenomenology. In the latter case the work tends to split between a behavioural determinism, often borrowing from evolutionary metaphor, and idealism; and this generic split between enclosure and liberation is the main subject of the present book. To the former I shall return in my conclusion.

These points may be put another way. Fowles's romances are deeply influenced by existentialism which, in its French form, has had a propensity for seeing the individual as either powerless victim or all-powerful god; either wholly subject to and determined by history or inventing those values which are to transcend history. Both of these views might well be thought partial and Romantic. As the critic John Bayley put it in 1966, 'the tenets of existentialism, apparently so pitiless and so searching, have become the opiate of the sub-intelligentsia, the props on which the common reader interested in ideas can comfortably recline' (*Tolstoy and the Novel*, p. 184). It is a real question for the Fowles critic as to what degree his writings are bound by such a limitation.

2

'THE COLLECTOR'

PAROLLES: Who cannot be crush'd with a plot? (*All's Well that Ends Well*, IV. iii)

Martin Green, in *The Children of the Sun* (London, 1977), has presented the case for reading twentieth-century English culture as a struggle between two consciences, each roughly identifiable with one of those poles of the middle class which are defined, with a sensitive line of demarcation between them, as on the one hand puritan and rigorous, on the other characterized by a stylishly playful and eccentric enjoyment of power. Thus on the one hand there is the nonconformist tradition with its severe hatred of false avowal and its ambition towards social equity, on the other the polymorphous and cynically latitudinarian ethos of the social establishment. Such a cultural division penetrated religion, education and the politics of literary culture itself, in which self-conscious modernism was often associated with a metropolitan *haute bourgeoisie*, while a conscientious realism was ascribed to writers for whom aesthetic and social opportunity were seen to be linked. The 1950s were the last decade in which these sets of alignment made for an urgent split. If the early post-war English novel has a characteristic hero, he has been figured as a provincial *arriviste* – the beneficiary, like his creator, of the 1944 Butler Education Act, who justly displaces or helps dilute the formerly hegemonic social establishment. Jim Dixon, at the peripeteia of Kingsley Amis's comic novel *Lucky Jim* (1954), wrestled with and outwitted the snobbish and inauthentic Bertrand Welch and magically won the girl, the job and the influence of London itself. The terrain of this hero was in two senses a parochial realism, in that the novels defined him against an unstrenuous regional history, the scenes of which (as in William Cooper's *Scenes from Provincial Life*, 1950) it patiently charted; but also because the technical means used to situate him there owed something to the deliberately provincial, technically uninquisitive naturalism of Wells or Trollope.

Bloomsbury novels had firmly relegated this hero to the edges of its imaginative vision. Charles Tansley, in Virginia Woolf's *To the Lighthouse* (1927), resented the condescensions of the host-culture and found its dialect impenetrable; he 'suspected its insincerity'. In Forster's *Howards End* (1910) a crueller lack of imaginative sympathy enabled Forster to allow the quarter-educated, culturally hungry Leonard Bast to die under a shower of books. He dies of a heart-attack brought on by the punishment of the privileged classes for having dared impregnate one of their number. It is an ungenerous irony that books – the very symbol of his aspiration – also mock him for seeking fulfilment outside his allotted place.

In *The Collector* (1963) the door to the cellar, in which the inadequate and deprived Clegg symbolically reverses the social order by imprisoning the privileged and hapless Miranda underground, is disguised by being lined with bookshelves. These bookshelves are accessible only to Clegg, for whom the word 'book' is often a euphemism for pornography, and are filled not with books but with tools, symbols of instrumentality and use. Clegg is in a sense the charmless great-nephew of Bast or the talentless younger brother of the classic 1950s hero, too witless to benefit from the new educational opportunities, too sensitive not to suffer his inadequacies ceaselessly. Empty tool-filled bookshelves, therefore, are a potently ironic symbol of one of the forces dividing England into two nations; and *The Collector*, in addressing itself to the politics of sexuality and social divisiveness, contrives to be a modest psychopathology of the age and its culture, as well as a sexual thriller.

*

The Collector had two sources. Fowles saw a performance of

Bartók's *Bluebeard's Castle* and was impressed by the symbolism of a man imprisoning women underground. He also read in the newspapers of a London boy who captured a girl and kept her three months in an air-raid shelter before her eventual escape (N). In its inception, therefore, the book owed something to myth as well as to history:

> It is the dramatic psychosexual implications of isolating extreme situations that excite and interest me. . . . In *The Collector* I tried to write in terms of the strictest realism; to go straight back to that supreme master of the fake biography Defoe, for the surface 'feel' of the book. To Jane Austen and Peacock, for the girl. To Sartre and Camus, for the 'climate'. ('I Write', p. 16)

'Realism' is attained partly through the use of the two first-person narrative voices of the protagonists; the author dispossesses himself by his own technical means, and the effect on the reader of reading two diary accounts of the same action creates the sense of a palimpsest. Each character narrates in their own dialect, and the mutual incomprehensibility of the two is a vital part of the effect. A great deal of care is evidenced in these social impersonations, and the skilful verisimilitude they create is responsible for the phantasmagoric intensity of the book as it approaches its macabre crisis.

Frederick Clegg is in his middle twenties, the self-pitying, mean-minded orphaned child of the lower middle classes, victim of an imaginatively stifling, emotionally repressive childhood, wounded in both his social and his sexual identity. He works in the rates department of the town hall annexe. He has sentimental and sadistic daydreams about Miranda Grey, whom, after sighting from the window, he subsequently spies on. His sole social outlet is with the 'Bugs' section of the local naturalist group where he discusses his butterfly collecting. Clegg logs Miranda's appearances ('she who ought to be wondered at', her name means in Latin) in his diary of entomological observations, as though she were an interesting, rare beetle, marking an 'X' until he learns her name, when he substitutes 'M'. His fantasies take on a new character when,

Gatsby-like, he wins a fortune on the football pools. He leaves his job, buys an old and remote house in Sussex, and an expensive camera and telephoto lens with which he photographs both his beloved butterflies and lovers coupling in the countryside. He captures Miranda, chloroforming her as he does his insects, and imprisons her in the room he has designed for her in the other world of the cellar. The parallels between Miranda and the butterflies are worked out in some detail.

Of the novel's four sections, the first two comprise the bulk of the book. Clegg's narrative provides the frame, and his account takes us, in the first section, up to a few days before Miranda's death; the novel then retraces the same events from Miranda's diary. The two brief final sections, like those of *The French Lieutenant's Woman*, each present a possible ending. The first is Clegg's fantasy: 'She was waiting for me down there. I would say we were in love, in the letter to the police. A suicide pact. It would be "The End".' The second gives the actual ending, in which we learn what Clegg's habit of referring to Miranda in the past tense throughout has prepared us for. Miranda dies of pneumonia; Clegg prepares for his next victim.

Throughout the book Clegg baulks Miranda's attempts to escape; accompanying and funding this action is the drama of incomprehension arising from the gaps and disjunctions between Clegg's and Miranda's narratives. Each of their texts deals in the received ideas of their class and in the platitudes that enshrine them. Unlike Dostoevsky's resentful Underground Man, another clerkly subversive, Clegg exemplifies infinitely more bad faith than he can attack, and he could be said at once to expose his own solipsism by failing to provide quotation marks for his own speech. The drama thus arises from what Nietzsche, in *The Genealogy of Morals*, terms 'the pathos of distance' – a phrase he invents to account for the social and ethical diversity of mankind and their putative single origin. This distance is not bridgeable by Miranda's policy of 'lame-ducking', and the book is in this sense a sad comedy of two opposed kinds of social inadequacy.

The rhetorical figure that characterizes Clegg's language is euphemism, that decorous imprecision which reveals a world in concealing it. He refers to Miranda not as his prisoner but as his guest. Death is 'The Great Beyond', and to murder is 'to put out'. A bikini is a 'Wotchermercallit' (when Miranda specifies it, he says 'I can't allow talk like that'). 'Nice' is a genteelism for non-sexual, garment for clothes; sex is 'the obvious' or 'the other thing', naked is 'stark', and 'artistic' often means pornographic. His language is impoverished, and sex produces the most hectic ellipses and periphrases:

> Well, of course with Aunt Annie and Mabel out of the way I bought all the books I wanted, some of them I didn't know such things existed, as a matter of fact I was disgusted, I thought here I am stuck in a hotel room with this stuff and it's a lot different from what I used to dream of about Miranda and me. (p. 14)

His ordinarily short, flat sentences twist about in the effort to accommodate their doubly inexpressible energies. Such an alienation from language means that he can blame it for his own criminality and achieve vertiginous effects of self-deception. So, while his imprisonment of Miranda is expressed merely as a form of eccentric hospitality, her undressing of herself is described as 'really shocking' (p. 109), and his photographic violation of her integrity at the book's core is simply 'what they call a culmination of circumstances' (p. 95) – after which perverse intimacy he cannot write a note to her beginning 'Dear Miranda' because it would be 'too familiar'. When she is dead he distances his guilt further by referring to her through the unctuous formality of 'The Deceased': the self-satisfied, primly bureaucratic derivativeness of the phrase typifies in its context Clegg's semi-literate talent for depersonalized vision, for anaesthetizing his imagination. 'Slimy' is the word he repeatedly uses for the indeterminate and inexpressible (pp. 11, 12, 16, 61), and it is appropriate, therefore, that he should imprison Miranda in the 'damp, nasty' place which itself encapsulates in its physical nature all that he disavows.

Clegg learns nothing, and indeed at the end is poised to enter the world of cyclical recurrence, which is also the world of myth, only this time with a girl who is not simultaneously a 'lady'. The puritan and destructive power of sexual idealism confused with gentility and male power is a commonplace symptom within the culture of the West – one within which women have long felt cruelly imprisoned and from which they increasingly urgently seek escape. Fowles addresses himself to it in all his books, and it feeds the major crisis in this, his first published novel, whose action is otherwise minimal. Clegg classically divides all women into whores ('specimens you'd turn away from, out collecting', p. 12), a category to which he has significantly been told his mother belonged; and *princesses lointaines* like Miranda, before whom he is ready to abase himself, rarities to be collected and worshipped. Clegg calls his capacity to wait 'old-fashioned' and notes that 'gentlemen control themselves' (p. 108). The tradition of courtly love, which presents the literary institutionalization of this confusion, is often embodied in romance, 'a story of sexual consummation delayed by events' (Scholes), and in which woman is often simultaneously satisfyingly unattainable yet ultimately magically enjoyable. *The Collector* refers insistently, like *The Magus*, to *The Tempest*, itself a species of romance and Fowles's favourite Shakespeare play. Though his real name is Frederick, Clegg presents himself to Miranda as Ferdinand, but is named by her in her diary as Caliban. Like Shakespeare's heroine, Miranda has attempts made on her virtue by her 'salvage and deformed slave' and awaits an impossible rescue. In Murdoch's *The Sea, The Sea*, another contemporary reworking of *The Tempest*, and an anti-romance (the consummation is not sexual) in which a man imprisons his ladylove (and where the social ironies work against the logic of courtly love), it is the Prospero figure who must learn to emancipate himself and, as in *The Magus*, reordain narrative propriety. *The Collector*, on the other hand, lacks any such educable and educative Prospero figure at its centre: Miranda's artist friend and mentor George Paston, who has some of the proper credentials, is himself at the edge of the action, and in any case himself treats Miranda as a mixture of *princesse lointaine* and Galatea to be manipulated. He belongs also to that world of 'history' commemorated in Miranda's diary as a world made inaccessible by the commencement of the mythic action.

Of Miranda, Fowles has said that she 'is an existentialist heroine although she doesn't know it. She's groping for her own authenticity. Her tragedy is that she will never live to achieve it. Her triumph is that one day she would have done so' (N, p. 255). If Clegg dehumanizes her by eroticizing her, she is equally unable to imagine his being. A 'nice little middle-class Doctor's daughter' (p. 257), she classifies his dialect as 'calibanese' and dramatizes her predicament as that of a member of the Few threatened by the Many. She sees herself as enshrining and preserving civilized values against what she snobbishly calls 'the new-class people with their cars and their money and their stupid vulgarities and their stupid crawling imitation of the bourgeoisie' (p. 218) – a view that Fowles (as he makes clear in *The Aristos*) endorses, with the qualification that 'The dividing line between the Few and the Many must run through each individual, not between individuals' (p. 9): each individual, being partly brutish as well as partly made of finer stuff, must struggle against the brute within himself as well as that within others. Like Clegg, Miranda is given to avoiding verbal 'impropriety', speaking of 'things from the chemist' (p. 227), 'time of the month' (p. 247), 'down the place' for lavatory, approvingly quoting the litotes 'fry-up' for nuclear holocaust, and deodorizing her language at various points ('I can't write what he said,' she says of an obscenity of Paston's); she even shares Clegg's 'the other thing' for sex, which is at one point 'crude' (p. 182). Like Clegg, too, she hates dirt, is an atheistical virgin with what she herself calls 'nasty perverted curiosity', refers to people by initials, uses cliché, and reifies Clegg by her scientific curiosity: 'Like you go to the zoo' (p. 76), he complains. While Clegg appears ineducable, however, Miranda is by no means so, and, indeed, had she not died 'might have become something better, the kind of being humanity so desperately needs' (*A*, p. 10).

Like Smithson in *The French Lieutenant's Woman* and Urfe in *The Magus*, she is stripped of presupposition and prejudice, 'loses her bearings' (p. 243); as with them too, this radical denuding of the spirit is the precondition for her access of good faith. The central irony of the book revolves around the action she takes as one consequence of her new-found self-awareness. For she offers herself to Clegg sexually, both to humanize and redeem him and to secure, she hopes, her own release. In making a gift of herself from whatever mixture of self-seeking and obverse sexual chivalry, she descends in Clegg's eyes from being a *princesse lointaine* to being one of what Clegg terms 'the other sort', from Virgin Mary to Eve, from hygienic female icon to incarnate seductress and whore. '*She had killed all the romance*' (p. 114; my italics), Clegg notes in the most demonic irony of the book. 'I didn't respect her any more, there was nothing left to respect. I knew her lark, no sooner she was up out of the room she was *as good as gone*' (p. 114; my italics). The contact she initiates with Clegg is one from which she probably catches the cold that, developing into untreated pneumonia, will kill her. The rhetoric of courtly love is again distantly and pejoratively echoed when the pro-nuclear-disarmament Miranda criticizes a USAF sergeant who thought that 'Americans were like knights of old rescuing a damsel in distress' (p. 144). Sexual idealism is a destructive force and a violently misleading metaphor.

*

Miranda reads Sillitoe's *Saturday Night and Sunday Morning* and criticizes the genre of proletarian pastoral to which it belongs for sentimentalizing the life of its (to her) Clegg-like hero, Arthur Seaton. (Sillitoe answered by creating, in *A Start in Life* (1970), another and very different Clegg.) It could be argued that what is attacked in *The Collector* is not working-class culture but the aesthetic dispensation under which its mimesis was felt as a primary obligation. 'Middle-class people are far more complex than working-class people' (C, p. 462), Fowles, begging a large number of questions, has asserted. But *The Collector* views *both* its characters, with a good deal of cold distance, as symptoms of the 'enormous genetic variety of life' (BBC), and as examples of Fowles's chilly talent for collecting and classifying the typical and the aberrant human specimen.

In the lengthy disquisitions on the role of the artist in society, as voiced through Miranda, the novel, though it has been claimed for realism, mounts an eloquent attack on that photographic naturalism which it is part of its own project to transcend. 'When you draw something it lives and when you photograph it it dies' (p. 58), Miranda preaches to Clegg. She does a number of drawings of a bowl of fruit, invites him to choose the best, and reviles him when he chooses merely the most lifelike. She explains that art is connected to the 'nasty' (p. 82), that it represents, in fact, exactly those parts of his psyche he has censored. 'You wouldn't imprison an innocent person if you [knew anything about art]' (p. 45), she asserts, defending a view of art as a species not merely of knowledge but of access to the highest truth. Moral improvement and the destruction of inferior art are indeed twice presented as analogous (pp. 126, 211), and it is consonant with this disdain for mere replication that she attacks Clegg's class as 'the horrid timid *copy-catting* genteel in-between class' (p. 172; my italics), and that even Clegg's lovemaking is to her 'just a desperate imitation of what he thinks the real thing's like' (p. 252). Clegg reflects Miranda's concern with art-as-truth when he corrupts her vocabulary by saying of the tied hands in a pornographic photograph he takes that they 'made an interesting motif' or that 'The best ones were with her face cut off' (p. 122).

Fowles has called *The Collector* a parable, and it is an impressive and not uncompassionate depiction of human evil, albeit one sometimes portentously scored. Just as Clegg reads 'Secrets of the Gestapo' and at first tells Miranda that he is 'only obeying orders' (p. 32), so Miranda's own chronicle of a young girl's moral growth, which, like that of a nursery plant, is 'forced', through her solitary confinement, is reminiscent of the Gestapo victim Anne Frank's – whose example, indeed, at one point Miranda invokes (p. 233). Critics who emphasize the book's warm and humane morality run the risk of prettifying its perceptions. It is in its own terms a 'nasty' work of art, which pays for its vision a characteristically modern price in dehumanization. 'I'm thinking of you as an object not as a person,' says Miranda, when trying to draw Clegg properly; indeed, it is part of the comfortless design of this novel that it turns its reader into a voyeur like Clegg,[20] perceiving the novel's agents as sexual and social objects, as well as subjects, involuntarily eavesdropping on two privacies. 'You're the one imprisoned in a cellar' (p. 62), Miranda tells Clegg; it is a cellar in which we too may be unwilling 'guests'. Fowles has come to a clearer understanding of this in recent years. 'That was a sort of cold-blooded book' (C, p. 456), he has said.

Fowles has related *The Collector* to Hardy's *The Well-Beloved*. In each case, Fowles argues, there is an irremediable authorial obsession with erotic loss. In *The Well-Beloved*, Hardy's last novel and a sort of metafiction about the sources of Hardy's creativity, the narrator – emotionally immature in a way that is artistically productive – falls in love with the same Ideal Woman whose spirit is reborn into three generations of women. His apparent earthly promiscuity is really an absolute loyalty to this Ideal Spirit. It is, Fowles argues, Hardy's inability in life to possess what this figure represents for him that caused his pained and obsessive return throughout his career to fictional embodiments; and Fowles – who confesses to innocent adolescent dreams of isolation with an admired girl which, though not criminal in his case, enabled him to approach Clegg with a degree of conviction – draws a parallel between the cyclical recurrence of *The Well-Beloved* and 'the way in which the monstrous and pitiable Clegg (the man who acts out his fantasies) prepares for a new "guest" in the Bluebeard's castle beneath his lonely house' ('Hardy', p. 38). The Persecuted Maidens of Fowles's later novels, we are invited to infer, are in some comparable sense reincarnations.

41

3

'THE MAGUS'

The romantic reaction . . . lacked a cult in which all men could take part. Instead it substituted imagination for reason and in place of the man of esprit *the artist as the priest-magician*. (W. H. Auden, *The Enchafed Flood* (my italics))

In the traditional romance no-one is ever disillusioned.
(Gillian Beer, *The Romance*)

The Magus is a compelling, grandly ingenious and oddly childlike book, as self-contradictory as a drawing by Maurits Escher. As in an Escher drawing, too, it is as impossible to hold the various illusory and mutually hostile fictional planes in a single comprehensible perspective as it is to separate them. A part of the satisfaction the book teasingly procures has comparably to do with the way it repeatedly sets up and then violates readerly expectation, encourages and then baffles interpretation, and refuses a point of rest to the mind's eye. Indeed, when at the end it seeks to secure such a closure, the reader, like the narrator, has been bewildered too effectively to feel entirely safe there – which may, too, be a part of the point.

The book opens and closes in a realistically depicted post-war Welfare State London, a world later seen as 'customary and habitable and orientated' (p. 495): a place of Fitzrovia Bohemians, Penguin *New Writing*, pony-tailed art students, duffel coats, beatniks, and the correspondent breeze of Marxist-entialism from the Left Bank over the Channel. The middle section depicts the difficult customary voyage of the epic hero into an underworld in search of a knowledge both arcane and usable. This *katabasis*, or literary descent, enacted on the Greek island of Phraxos, involves spectacular theatrical mys-tifications, a flamboyantly improbable psychodrama. Beginning on the conjuror's estate Bourani, it gradually colonizes the rest of the island, southern Europe and finally that London in which the book began. Both this 'London' and the technical means by which it was presented are at the end infected with the illusion and mystery whose controlling origin was one corner of the island – a contamination that partly also requires to be read as a secular redemption.

The book's paradoxes have kept Fowles busy, on and off, over a quarter of a century. It was the first novel he wrote, in the early fifties, interrupting it for various projects including *The Collector*. He felt its publication in 1965 to have been premature, and he revised and reissued it in 1977. Given Fowles's commitment to open-endedness, and his odd relations with this novel, there seems no reason why this should be the last revision. Indeed, the title-story of *The Ebony Tower* was itself 'a kind of realistic version of *The Magus*' which had been 'altogether too full of mystery' (R). He has consistently spoken of the book as the one that succeeds the least well but of which he remains the most fond: 'I like the worst best' (*JML*, p. 186). It is 'a great sprawling monster . . . closer to my heart than *The Collector*' (UEA), 'this wretched book' (S, p. 32), and he spoke of it to Richard Boston as a failure: 'I hadn't the technique. The form is inadequate to the content' (B). It is none the less the book that has aroused more interest than anything else he has written, and he suggests that this may be due to the fact that it is 'a novel of adolescence written by a retarded adolescent' (*MR*, p. 9).

Fowles cites three possible influences. It was in a sense 'a re-working of *Le Grand Meaulnes*' (C, p. 457); the original draft, with a clearer supernatural element, owed something to James's *The Turn of the Screw*; and *Great Expectations* was, he later saw, an unconscious influence. All three cunningly turn on prevarications about the nature of illusion. *Le Grand Meaulnes* (sometimes translated as *The Lost Domain*), the one completed novel of Henri Alain-Fournier (1886–1914), is a haunting fiction of double erotic quest and loss – a romantic novel which, like *The Magus*, triumphantly refuses maturity, yearningly mourns the failure of the uncompromising emotions of childhood at the same time that it magically asserts the terrible pathos of their ascendancy. A lost, and at first nameless, domain is the focus for this emotion, a place of illusion about which the story's stout-hearted, adolescent playfellows can dream and scheme. *The Turn of the Screw*, James's best-known novella, is a chilling ghost story in the gothic mode and also a study in epistemological scepticism – which is to say an exploration of the ways in which experience itself refuses easy decoding and appears quixotically to license each individual to construct his own world out of the materials available to him. *Great Expectations*, a classical realist *Bildungsroman*, presents the maturation and sentimental education of Pip. *The Magus* is a novel about education, inside a very different kind of novel, which ironizes the world in which *Bildungsromane* can still be written.

*

Just as Pip was a quintessentially inauthentic gentleman of the mid-Victorian epoch, so a century later the hero of *The Magus* is, Fowles points out, 'a typical inauthentic man of the 1945–50 period' (C, p. 466); in both books first-person narrative inducts us directly into both the hero's bad faith and an imaginative understanding of his consequent reform. *Great Expectations* is about the destruction of illusion; *The Magus* is also about the complicity of all fiction in illusion, a complicity from which it tries to shake itself free. Nicholas Urfe, like Pip, is an orphan and, unlike him (though like Clegg in *The Collector*, and also like Sarah and Charles in *The French Lieutenant's Woman*), is also an orphan without brothers or sisters. Fowles's attraction to the siblingless orphan protagonist [21] is a function of his attraction to rationalistic fable and to a model of reality depending heavily on the romantic rhetoric of the heroic moment of lonely individual choice.

Urfe is a middle-class Oxford graduate, a poetaster given to portentous vapourings (his name links him with the seventeenth-century French writer of pastoral romance, d'Urfé), a chilly narcissist and apprentice dandy, a second-rate Lothario who romanticizes his shabby commonplace treatment of women as 'crimes' (p. 21) and a hollow man who has learnt at Oxford to dignify his attitudinizings as 'existentialist' (p. 17). He grandly perceives himself as an original and an 'exile' from 'the mass-produced middle-class world' from which he comes. He starts to live with Alison Kelly, an Australian girl also in a sense orphaned by emigration. She has some talent for truth and freedom and, despite seeing through Urfe's emotional dishonesty, falls in love with him. 'You say you're isolated,' she tells him, 'but you really think you're different' (p. 35). For him she is something to be used if nothing better turns up, and, failing to understand the real nature of their connection, he gets a job as schoolmaster on a remote Greek island, Phraxos. The name is related to the Greek word for design or plan.[22] Here the 'onanistic literary picture' he maintains of himself causes him to blame the world of the school for the failure of his verse, and believing himself to have syphilis, and in a rapture of self-pity and self-dislike, he stages an unsuccessful suicide attempt. There does not seem to be enough of him to kill.

Urfe is romantically given to picturing his ego asserting itself against a pedestrian and inhospitable world, a place deeply hostile to 'originality' and self-effectuation. At this stage he describes his existential situation as follows:

> Years later I saw a *gabbia* at Piacenza: a harsh black canary-cage strung high up the side of the towering campanile, in which prisoners were left to starve to death and rot in full view of the town below. And looking up at it I remembered that winter in Greece, that *gabbia* I had constructed for myself out of light, solitude and self-delusions. (p. 62)

This self-imposed romantic incarceration prefigures the opposing liberating/imprisoning magical enclosure of Bourani, where Urfe will discover a world that educationally resists the self yet enhances its sense of its uniqueness. The book deals in a chain of such islanded estates, beginning with Britain itself, which is at both the beginning and the end a *gabbia*, yet a potentially magical island too.

After swimming off the cape on which the eccentric millionaire Maurice Conchis has his villa, Urfe finds that a verse anthology has been planted underneath a neighbouring towel, with passages marked for his edification. He has the sensation – a recurrent one – of being watched.

> We shall not cease from exploration
> And the end of all our exploring
> Will be to arrive where we started
> And know the place for the first time.

This passage from T. S. Eliot's 'Little Gidding', a *mise-en-abîme*, an encapsulation of the moral action of the book which epitomizes its tendentious circularity, is the first of a series of passages, a dozen or so of which concern islands or the sea. (The lesson of Donne's best-known sermon waits here in the wings.) When he meets Conchis he is mysteriously expected. 'I chose well?' asks Conchis, signifying both his villa in its beautiful setting and also that mystique of choice in which he will show himself an adept.

Conchis is at one level the twentieth-century metaphysical equivalent of a Cheeryble or a Brownlow, those rich and anachronistically feudal Dickensian dispensers of authorial providence. He refers to himself as Prospero, explains that Bourani means both 'skull' and 'gourd', and begins the story of his life, a story whose telling occupies much of the narrative space of the book. He talks a perfect but odd English – he was born and brought up in England – full of a metaphysical innuendo reminiscent, especially in the revised version, of the mystagogy of *The Aristos*. He asks Urfe whether he feels elect and tells him, 'Hazard makes you elect. You cannot elect yourself' (p. 87). Art objects teach Urfe respect for Conchis, who possesses a Modigliani, two Bonnards, an original Pleyel harpsichord and a fifteenth-century Venetian colonnade to his house which is reminiscent of Fra Angelico's *The Annunciation*. Art authenticates Conchis for Urfe and disturbs his own sense of mastery. Conchis describes a painting by Bonnard as 'giving the whole of existence a reason' (like the 'little song'

46

Roquentin hears at the end of Sartre's *La Nausée*). All these art objects, we later learn, are fake. Conchis's library consists mainly of biography and autobiography – those post-Reformation *catalogues raisonnées* of the evolution of the substantial self, of the exposure of a nascent identity to the vindication of God or history. He hates and has burned all the novels he has owned: 'Words are for truth. For facts. Not fiction' (p. 96). He lends Urfe a book of photographs of female breasts, informs him he is psychic, measures his skull with calipers, and expounds the doctrine of mystic voluntarism according to which each individual must recognize that his life contains a moment, like a peripeteia in fiction, for potential self-coincidence, for being and not becoming.

Urfe takes to weekending at Bourani and is the rapt audience to Conchis's life-story, a history of extremities and adventures of the will, which he sensationally relates to that 'Jungian collective Id of Europe', the plot of history itself. Shortly Urfe finds that Conchis's narrations are prefigured or echoed by a series of bizarre apparitions promiscuously mixing up myth and history, private and public. Conchis's ordeal in the trenches in the First World War is preceded by an imposture with loaded dice and cyanide-filled human molars, after which Urfe hears 'Tipperary' sung and smells putrefaction. Such vicarious participation in Conchis's narration makes Urfe a peculiarly privileged 'reader'. No hypothesis naturalizes these phenomena, which he describes as 'in some way fictional'. Conchis asks Urfe merely to 'pretend to believe', and then catches and kills an octopus which mistakes a piece of sheet for bait, as if demonstrating the possible cost of exactly such credulousness. Hearing and smell having been beguiled, Urfe now sees the seventeenth-century writer of a pamphlet he has been reading. Later again he sees Lily, Conchis's dead fiancée, or her ghost, or an actress portraying her.

Urfe visits Athens and rejoins Alison for a few days, but jilts her again. He has begun to fall in love with Lily, who, unlike Alison, appears to be another magical virgin whom he can safely idealize, as Clegg idealized Miranda. She satisfies his nostalgia for that 'extinct Lawrentian woman of the past, the woman inferior to man in everything but that one great power of female dark mystery and beauty' (p. 242). Alison, by contrast, is the 'good-time girl' whom he discounts, since she is, like a man (as Urfe sees it), in touch with her own sexual needs in a way that is dangerous for him. He returns to the 'polysemantic world' of Bourani. From this point a Jamesian series of turns of the screw, of calculated shocks and reversals, successively require and defeat new explanation. Each time Urfe is sure he has reached the truth, this, in turn, is shown to be merely a trick performed by Conchis; who, like a Zen master, sets up and smashes illusion. Urfe has found himself in an addictively satisfying maze, and his quest appears endless. Conchis is a lover of the curious, an ornithologist, a psychic, a 'polyhedral character', a presenter of baroque private masques which are a 'strange new meta-theatre', an entrepreneur, musician, psychiatrist, charlatan, shaman, an absconded god, a necromancer, an 'Empson of the event', hypnotist, a Gatsby who once held fine parties, a Svengali, an existentialist hero who understands and wishes to initiate others into the cruelty of freedom. No theory about him coheres. Lily is a ghost, then a romantically imprisoned schizophrenic, then an actress who is the victim of Conchis's corrupt theories, or alternatively their just instrument . . . She wishes to defect to Urfe's camp . . . Her defection is itself a part of the plot . . .

*

At one point Urfe suggests that the English as a race are uniquely duplicitous, adept at the polite mask and the polite perfidy (p. 372). Immediately after this, Urfe and Lily are outwitted by Conchis, the implication being that even their duplicities are amateurish compared with his Europeanized ones. The theme of English ontological virginity, as it were, has important consequences, for the crisis in Conchis's story is the choice he is offered as mayor of Phraxos during the Nazi occupation – of killing three Resistance fighters and saving many lives, or dying along with eighty hostages. He chooses to die in a moment of moral vision he would like to transmit to

48

Urfe. Conchis's plottings and Urfe's counter-plottings – detections that are themselves, as it turns out, circumscribed and belong to the world of predictive form that Conchis has created – each lead up to this evocation of Conchis's moment of wartime choice. It has been pre-haunted by an elaborate episode involving German soldiers on the island's central ridge, during which Urfe is charged with being a traitor. Sexual and political treachery are linked, and Urfe has learnt that, as a consequence of the first, Alison has killed herself. The world in which this occurred and the world of Nazi-occupied Phraxos are both 'a man's world. . . . Men see objects, women see the relationship between objects' (p. 413) (men are existentialists, women structuralists, Scholes wittily glosses this). The chapter of Conchis's choice is the only one with a heading, the Greek word for freedom (*eleutheria*).

It is worth digressing here to recall that Sartrean existentialism drew heavily on a folklore derived from the Second World War. Making inwardness a function of action, and perceiving the will as always *in extremis*, it was in a sense a philosophy of mobilization which memorialized engagement. The type of the inauthentic man was surely the quisling, the man whose internal contradictions were so dramatically consequential. Existentialism in this form, it might be said, was a doctrine of subjective absolutism made for a world operatically void (unlike art) of any prevenient design, and with a special relevance for the apocalyptic events of the 1940s, in which men could be divided into collaborators and *Maquisards*. Sartre's *Existentialism and Humanism* (1946) had as its central *exemplum* a young man divided between looking after his mother and joining the Resistance – divided (as Smithson is also to be) between choosing the past or the future. Urfe has been initiated into the century's grandest and most horrible mystery.

That 'true freedom which lies between each two' (p. 10) is the object of Urfe's quest, but before he is deemed ready to test out his capacities for it he is tested again himself – first by Lily's two abscondings, one before, one after sex; then by an elaborate mock-trial in which the actors in Conchis's masque have renounced any claim to belong to his autobiography and are dressed as figures from myth who talk psychiatric jargon. They definitively unmask Urfe's pretensions, classifying and reifying him as merely 'typical' in his inadequacies. He is now given a whip and offered the chance of revenging his humiliations on Lily's bared back. Understanding that this choice mirrors Conchis's when confronted with the mutilated terrorists in the war, he refuses. He is now forced to watch Lily in a pornographic film, then sees her make love with a Negro in his presence. He has been stripped morally and readied for that despair which is one prerequisite for good faith. He is now (apparently) set free and learns that Alison's suicide had been faked: she too has joined Conchis's troupe. Urfe struggles to make sense of what has happened to him, devising elaborate tests of the 'truthfulness' of his experiences. He finds that Conchis apparently died four years before he met him. As he 'died' twice before, this new death may be in kind.

In London he meets the real Lily, Conchis's childhood friend and, confusingly, the mother of the actress Lily. He treats two new friends with ordinary kindness: Jo-Jo, a Glaswegian waif, with whom he has brotherly relations; Kemp, an ageing Bohemian whom he permits to mother him. As Scholes puts it, he has thus symbolically rejoined the human family, most of whom appear also to be Conchis's creatures; he is ready to be confronted with Alison in the flesh, and a future they may or may not share. Alison's name, he has learnt, means 'without madness'.

*

At one level, Conchis's nearest parallel is Prospero, the magically virtuous enslaver with whom he explicitly identifies himself. Thus he sets Urfe Ferdinand-like tasks, and references to *The Tempest* and to chess abound throughout. The world of Shakespeare's late romances is cavalier about probabilities, playful about credulousness and interested in illusion-as-miracle. Nicholas Brooke has argued of *The Tempest* that

> After a sensational opening, relatively simple tricks build up towards the full-scale masque . . . and after that has been

dismissed, the technics of magic are progressively abandoned. The last 'show' of Miranda and Ferdinand playing chess is at once miraculous to the stage-audience (who do not know that they are alive) and entirely natural to us (who do). It therefore *reverses the process of illusion.* (my italics)[23]

The Magus also uses illusion in order to disillusion, but foregrounds its formal anxieties about doing so. After a quiet opening, the relatively simple tricks lead up to Conchis's anguished choice in the war, with its complicated and expensive pre-haunting with special German actors; and the 'show' of Miranda and Ferdinand playing chess is paralleled by the 'show' of the live Alison in an Athenian taxi which appears to Urfe who, like the reader, had thought her dead. It is a show that also alludes to the educational fake-deaths of *A Winter's Tale* and *Much Ado About Nothing.*

As in *The Tempest*, however, where the reform of characters so ingeniously befuddled seems highly gestural (the usurper Antonio never recants on stage), so in *The Magus*. Scholes makes an elegant case for reading the book as Urfe's renunciation of both dishonesty and literal-mindedness, a renunciation theatrically induced by Conchis's calculatedly dishonest exploitation of credulity. At the end, we are asked to understand, Urfe can at last distinguish 'life' from 'literature'. This reading safeguards an oddly nineteenth-century sense of moral space and perspective within the novel, one that Fowles's revisions of the book importantly emphasize: playing down the occult, cutting out the dedication to Astarte and the epigraph from *The Key to the Tarot*, strengthening the autonomy of Lily in particular, and making the ending more didactic.[24] *The Magus* is to do what novels in the past have so often done: to enact or point to a secular redemption, relating the learning and unlearning of a biography to the manifest irreversibilities of history itself.

Fowles has said that he wished in *The Magus* to provide, as *Le Grand Meaulnes* does, 'an experience beyond the literary' (*MR*, p. 6); and also that '*The Magus* was of course a deliber-

51

ately artificial, model-proposing novel, a good deal more about fiction than any "real" situation' (ZB, p. 120). The instinctiveness with which he sought a balance between a book that mediated such an extraliterary experience, and one that simultaneously questioned the conventions on which such an experience must be based, was indicated when he said 'It really wasn't a literary experience writing that book – it was much more psychological and emotional' (UEA). He intended Conchis to 'exhibit a series of masks representing human notions of God, from the supernatural to the jargon-ridden scientific; that is, a series of human illusions about something that does not exist in fact, absolute knowledge and absolute power' (p. 10). In Scholes's reading, Urfe's liberation from illusion involves his orbital insertion into the world of hermetic mysteries, after which he can be safely returned to an emblematic 'real world', indemnified in future against artistic or crypto-theological interference. Such a reading privileges those *topoi* in which Urfe demonstrates his waxing ability to distinguish 'art' from 'life', which in turn are to lead to a fictionalist vanishing-point or world at the end of the rainbow where art and theology both reveal their defencelessness, and where a moral perspective, newly vitalized, at last coheres. It involves a subordination – one that Fowles's revisions make quite clear he intended – of the illusionistic delays, the turns of the fictionalist screw, to the realistic conclusion; it seeks what the first version in a give-away moment of neurotic hyperbole called a moment of 'final, ultimate, absolute truth' (p. 386). Even in the revised version such a place of dangerous safety – the 'unfakable truth' (p. 418) – is threatened by an aporetic backwash or leakage from the god-game itself, a world whose limits (Urfe calls it 'a world without limits') are for ever in question. Thus the last chapter is rendered even more peculiar than most of Fowles's last chapters. Its first paragraph has his earliest pronounced metalepsis – a deliberate disjunction in the text caused by moving from one narrative level to another. Here the text jolts out of the first person into an entirely new third-person narrative voice which, entranced by its own lyricism, struggles to 'free' Urfe through the paradox of making his autarky the function of a long intertextual past. And the present tense, the tense of eternal instantaneity in which the revised version finally suspends Alison, is immolation as much as emancipation. These are clear attempts to disintoxicate the reader, and comparable to the way in which Conchis tries to force Urfe to wither into the truth.

'I'm not quite sure what the difference is between what you're doing here and the thing you hate so much – fiction,' says Urfe at one point (p. 231); and he is answered, 'I do not object to the principles of fiction. Simply that in print, in books, they remain mere principles.'

Conchis is also an avant-garde but omniscient novelist, who, naturally, suspects novels. *The Magus* in this sense is a meta-novel about 'realism': the novelist has been inserted into his book so that we can monitor his compassionate sadism at work. Conchis is omnipresent by the end as well as dead, has used 'pre-hauntings' and echoes which are narrative prefigura-tions and recurrences, and tries to establish interpretative levels of narration which he authenticates by skilful use of 'local colour' and 'period detail'. The 'smile', which, like the 'slap', is just such a mysterious recurrence as Urfe is to be initiated into, is described at one point as a dramatic irony, which is to say a privileged knowledge about the unfolding of the plot. Conchis distributes allusions, puns, parables, and illustrations to his text. He provides Urfe with an anagnorisis (the trial-scene in which Urfe fully 'knows' himself) and a sensational series of peripeteias, among which two are meant to stand out: his betrayal by Lily and Alison's reappearance. He then sets his character free, returning him to a world where he has indicated he will not be watching. This Conchis novelist is perhaps not a very good writer, and has his own credulities about metaphor; but, like Fowles himself, he has a splendid and seductive narrative drive. Fowles in his Preface nudges our attention to the 'significant' quotation at the end from the *Pervigilium Veneris* (the 'Eve of the Festival of Love') in Late Latin which might be translated 'Tomorrow let him love who has never loved; and he who has loved, let him tomorrow love'; like Fowles, Conchis is a remorseless pedagogue, quixotic about sharing his expertise.

The most crucially and oddly balanced passage in the book is the one in which the disenchanted and now bravely honest Urfe says:

> All my life I had turned life into fiction, to hold reality away; always I had acted as if a third person was watching and listening and giving me marks for good and bad behaviour – a god like a novelist, to whom I turned like a character with the power to please, the sensitivity to feel slighted, the ability to adapt himself to whatever he believed the novelist-god wanted. This leech-like variation of the super-ego I had created myself, fostered myself, and because of it I had always been incapable of acting freely. It was not my defence; but my despot. And now I saw it, I saw it a death too late. (p. 539)

The structural ambiguity of the book, which reflects Fowles's 'peculiar moral ambiguity' (*JML*, p. 231), is exposed here with dizzying effect. Certain critics tell us that Urfe's delusion that he is being watched is Sartrean bad faith. He *is* being watched, of course. There *is* a novelist-god whom he pleases and displeases, and also a leech-like variant of the superego (a modern version, of course, partly disguised as the id), designed – like George Eliot's *œuvre* – to correct the faults of the bourgeois English. A procession of English schoolmasters reaching back decades have been worked on by Conchis before Urfe; an American follows him; Conchis's method is powerless against totalitarians like Urfe's immediate predecessor Mitford. *The Magus* is an extended attack on the use of literature as sympathetic magic; and also one of its grandest exemplifications.

*

There is, of course, a contemporary artistic cult of impasse itself, in which the writer is praised, as John Barth praised Borges, for confronting 'an intellectual dead end and employ[ing] it against itself to accomplish new human work' (*NT*,

p. 76). In post-modernism it is its own deep necessary formal illogic that becomes art's principal subject-matter. What distinguishes *The Magus*, I should wish to suggest, is, as much as the rescue of realism by the world of fictional hypothesis, the obsessive hounding of romance and its subjection to the requirement of authentication – a demand that makes it perpetually, proteanly elude capture and adopt new shapes. Gillian Beer has described such emancipations of realism by romance and shown, too, that they impose between author and reader a relationship that 'liberates but also involves unusual dependency'.[25] This dependency in *The Magus*, exemplified by Urfe and shared by his reader, is put at the service of a programme, like that systematic confusion proposed by Daniel to his young soldier in *Les Chemins de la liberté*, which is scarcely less bleakly self-regarding than what it replaces.

Urfe early identifies his sense of reality with gravity, perhaps echoing Nietzsche's prescient observation that the death of God makes all weightless. A crucial early hallucination, hypnotically induced, teaches him that he was 'not looking up, but down into space, as one looks into a well' (p. 237). Like Dante in *The Inferno*, disorientated by crossing the Devil's privates, he passes a moral-gravitational frontier. If in *The Collector* the contest between the two texts increased the illusion of a tiny but sharable space between them, exemplifying a Jamesian law of successive aspects, in *The Magus* the succession of phenomenological aspects accretes a spiralling series of vertiginous spaces (comparable to a switchback, or to op art) which please yet dismay. This Rimbaudian *dérèglement des sens* – the epigraphs suggest that they are also Sadian ethical denudations – flatters as well as releasing the self. At the beginning, Urfe is a romantic solitary who 'rejects his own age'. In the middle, while learning 'to be what he is', he again pictures reality scornfully as 'a steady job and a house in the suburbs'. By the end he is not merely homeless but *species-less* too – a claim for himself (twice repeated) that is even more magniloquent than any he made at the start. Freedom, that existentialist's *ignis fatuus*, is, in the penultimate chapter, still 'making some abrupt choice and acting on it; was as it had been at Oxford, allowing one's instinct-cum-will to fling one off at a tangent, solitary into a new situation' (p. 643). He is still a romantic solitary, still split between idealism and determinism, oscillating between a specious despair at his emptiness and an equally facile Luciferian exaltation at his capacity for levitation and escape.

The masque, we recall, is a courtly entertainment, flattering to privilege, and the god-game confers 'a uniqueness on me'. Sartrean existentialism, which denounces the man who holds himself 'necessary', is given to an odd sleight-of-hand: he who thinks himself 'necessary' is a *bourgeois salaud* and damned. He who understands his own contingency, who is an intimate of the forces of hazard, is mysteriously on the way to having his bad faith purged and to becoming, like an art-work, necessary again. It conceals a doctrine of secret election. The bourgeois self of a failed artist (Urfe) is attacked, and what ideally replaces it is a concealed version of that most highly evolved of selves, the great artist: that finally authenticated demiurge fantasticating in his void. Here, for all his disclaimers, the artist is Conchis, who by creating his 'novel' with live actors partakes of a full moral ambiguity. Like Clegg, he uses a camera to reify, and also collects human specimens. He is surrounded by art objects of dubious provenance. Like De Deukans, he is an explicitly corrupt Des-Esseintes-like collector of collections; unlike Henrik Nygaard, the paranoiac who finds interconnection everywhere, Conchis uses connection in his masque to expose its absence elsewhere. The art object he creates is a paradoxically paranoiac universe itself, predetermined even when its *telos* is to denounce teleology and reveal mystery. The secret meaning of De Deukans's and Nygaard's simultaneous demise may be a Jungian trope about the simultaneity of a-causal phenomena; it also points to an equivalence between aesthete and paranoiac, for both of whom, as for the neo-Platonic priest-mage, 'All teems with symbol; the wise man is the man who in any one thing can read another' (Plotinus, *Enneads*). For both, as for Virginia Woolf, 'the whole world is a work of art ... we are parts of the work of art'.[26] For neo-symbolist art as for theodicy there can be no spare moments: each detail is irradiated with intention. There can in one sense be no level at which Urfe is not being watched: the book has equivocated too cleverly to be able to assert one.

*

At one point Conchis – who, we are to learn, 'used to give a famous lecture on art as institutionalised illusion' – speaks of the audience for a pamphlet he wrote on 'Communication Intermondiale'. 'Did you get any response from your pamphlet?'

> A great deal. From the wrong people. From the miserable vultures who prey on the human longing for the solution of the final mysteries. The spiritualists, the clairvoyants, the cosmopaths, the summer-landers, the blue-islanders, the apportists – all that *galère*. (p. 235)

This conversation now seems prophetic. For all its attacks on occultism and the false consolations of religious authority, one of the apt ironies of *The Magus*'s reception has been the audience it has shared with Hesse, Tolkien and Casteneda. It has found its most appreciative audience among the celebrants of otherworldly carnival in which the decade of desperate optimism and of its first publication abounded. Just as Urfe fights a battle against self-deception, so the book in which he fights it struggles to prevent its own moral spaciousness collapsing into 'the one banal, inexhaustible concept'[27] of the fiction of infinite regress and festive indeterminacy. Neither struggle is conclusive. In this sense the book uses a hugely audacious pathetic fallacy to correct a local one. Ruskin in *Modern Painters* suggested that this fallacy, by which all nature is humanized, or egotized, is peculiar to prophets 'perceiving realities too strong for men to bear' and second-order poets 'whose emotions are too strong for their intellects'. *The Magus* might be said to be the prophetic history of such a second-order poet, and colludes with the kinds of vision it is wistful about correcting.

4

'THE FRENCH LIEUTENANT'S WOMAN'

A text always has several epochs and reading must resign itself to that fact. And this genealogical self-representation is itself already the representation of a self-representation; what, for example, 'the French eighteenth century', if such a thing existed, already constructed as its own source and its presence. (Jacques Derrida, *Of Grammatology*)

In Borges' witty fable 'Pierre Menard, Author of the Quixote', Menard, an early twentieth-century French novelist, is inspired to compose or re-create unseen several chapters of Cervantes' novel. He wishes to transcend both 'the plebeian pleasures of anachronism' and the banal enthralling of the reader with the 'elementary idea that all epochs are the same or are different'. When he has completed his fragment, the narrator explicates it, demonstrating that, while the words on the page are identical in Cervantes and Menard, *Menard's text is the more subtle*. The soft and slippery problems of historical and aesthetic relativism are Fowles's special province in his most important novel. Like Borges, he is concerned with the ways in which the self, like the text, is a locus of permanent change, with how both live in and are subject to history. Fowles has been criticized for pretending to write in *The French Lieutenant's Woman* the nineteenth-century novel that century forgot to produce, for trying to be a popular novelist of the nineteenth century a hundred years too late. Just as John Barth has pointed out that if Chartres Cathedral were rebuilt today it could only be done ironically, so *The French Lieutenant's Woman* is just such a would-be ironized structure, utilizing the 'plebeian pleasures of anachronism' to throw into creative relief the narrative conventions and cultural presuppositions of each epoch.

Fowles's first three novels can each be read as a palimpsest, foregrounding a textual contest in which one constituent discourse is angled towards historical survival, not always meritoriously. In *The Collector* Miranda and Clegg's diaries offset one another, and one future (Clegg's) overwhelms another. In *The Magus* the realist text of Urfe's life is subjected to a possibly redemptive struggle with the post-modernist text of Conchis's, who pertinently interweaves his supposed narrative past with Urfe's narrative present. *The French Lieutenant's Woman* contains Fowles's most ambitious battle of the styles and his most ironic truce. Here the contest and transaction are between a pastiche nineteenth-century text and the epoch of its composition a century later, in relation to which the text stands as a Conchis-like pre-haunting, interwoven therefore with a future which it only partly predicates but which has necessarily produced it. Fictional illusionism is constantly intensified by an authorial presence more openly and busily obtrusive than that of *The Magus*, and playing on the double temporality of the story and the narrating: playing persistently, that is, on the obscure gap between the world in which the telling is done and the world of which it tells.

Fowles has given a valuable account of the novel's genesis. He was imaginatively solicited by the figure of a woman staring out to sea from a deserted quay ('Notes').[28] She represented a reproach to the Victorian age – she declined to belong to another epoch – and is an outcast. Like Lucy Hughes in J. G. Farrell's *The Siege of Krishnapur* (1973), a novel set in 1857, Sarah Woodruff is a *femme incomprise*. Unlike Lucy – who, despite being seduced by a soldier and despite her early histrionics about being a 'fallen woman', enjoys both sex and flirting and ends by cheerfully marrying a general – Sarah will defy the age that declines to accommodate her. Fowles did not think of his book at first as a historical novel – itself, of course, a classically Victorian genre, and a genre in which he has very little interest. He none the less makes it clear that he is divided between the desire to write a Victorian novel and the desire to expose the pretence on which such an ambition must be based: between inhabiting the literary pieties of the old tradition and demonstrating a felt obligation towards the ironic and self-conscious wisdom of his own age. He is thus necessarily interested in the creative possibilities of anachronism; trying to put the dialogue of one chapter into contemporary English, he finds that this generates untoward comedy. He also tries rendering a dialogue faithfully '1867' (in so far as it can be heard in books of the time) but finds that this sounds insufficiently old-fashioned: not stiff or euphemistic enough 'to agree with our psychological picture of the Victorians'. Clearly his aim is not to disturb our psychological picture of the Victorians but to flatter it and put it to work for his own purposes. The speech he invents is consciously archaic, to accord with this folklore. An important part of his purpose is to show two Victorians making love, something he compares with science fiction. He sets his book in the year in which the first volume of Marx's *Kapital* appeared, in which the British Parliament passed the Second Reform Bill, and during which Mill campaigned for the emancipation of women; in which, indeed, both the sexual politics against which we are still reacting, and the relative stability of the Victorian synthesis itself, were beyond their point of highest confidence and showing signs of breaking up.

About this synthesis Fowles suggests that, until Darwin and Lyell helped expose the new post-theological space–time continuum, 'man had lived in a small room' ('Notes', p. 140) – an image developed within the novel when he writes of Victorian claustrophilia. The mid-nineteenth century is the last, most paradoxical and impressively documented of Fowles's many enclosed spaces: a pre-lapsarian womb of repressive conventionality from which humankind will be excluded as from Eden and simultaneously liberated as from gaol. It is that alleged 'golden age of repression' which Michel Foucault so ironizes in *The History of Sexuality*. As Huffaker notes, a Fall myth underlies the novel. Charles acts it out, but the compositional problem precisely mirrors it. As a contemporary English novel-

60

ist, Fowles is exemplarily split between the temptation to be an epigone deferring to a falsely innocent tradition and that of being a free but fallen solipsist seeking a new one. The garden into which he cannot return is formal as much as historical. He thus makes structural to the novel the problem of so many post-war British novelists – how to reconstitute the usable elements of nineteenth-century realism – but he brings to the programme some paradoxically Victorian gifts of his own: 'there is something sadly shallow and blinded in our age' is a Carlylean note sounded elsewhere than in *The French Lieutenant's Woman* ('Notes'), as a glance at *The Aristos*, where Fowles equally easily impersonates a patriarchal and sententious omniscience, will show. One of the Borges-like ironies of *The French Lieutenant's Woman* is that Fowles creates for himself a complex form which both exploits his best writerly gifts yet provides a neutralizing and ironic habitat for his vices. His extraordinary narrative drive and love of plot, his taste for *facetiae*, sentimental melodrama, neo-gothic sensationalism, cant, and his competing desire to research the substantiality of the self – all, like cuckoos, find a hospitable and consciously foreign nest.

For two centuries the form of romance we call gothic has funded a major source of opposition to realism. After the late eighteenth century, when secondary writers developed the mode, this impolite form enjoyed different revivals in both the 1860s, in which *The French Lieutenant's Woman* is set, and the 1960s, in which it was written. The 'sensation novel' of the 1860s,[29] with its emphasis on tangled intrigue, mysterious past passions and melodramatic confrontations, and its fascination with the actual psychology of sensation, influenced not merely Dickens and Wilkie Collins but writers whose talents and sensibility might have been thought to lie outside it: Trollope, Charlotte Yonge, George Eliot, the early Hardy. A century later, British writers such as Iris Murdoch, Beryl Bainbridge, Angela Carter and Elaine Feinstein each turned differently to gothic to fulfil needs the realist tradition could not satisfy. While realism could be seen as a pastoral form in that the assumptions behind its technical means depended on nostalgic simplification, wantonly faking up an easy continuity with the past, gothic on the other hand problematizes and destabilizes the otherwise smooth filiation between past and present. It reveals continuity itself to be disjunctive, a form of violence or revenge perpetrated by the past (the guilty secret, the unshriven crime) on the present, and it points to a broken lineage, an alienation of each from the other. The world again splits between idealism and determinism, between ghostly capture and supernatural escape.

The French Lieutenant's Woman arrives at gothic in two senses. Like the sensation novel of the 1860s, its plot is highly melodramatic and manipulates tension to brilliant effect, as it approaches its due violation of culturally sanctioned areas of secrecy in the form of the sexual act between Charles and Sarah. That journalism of the emotions which in *The Collector* produced

> Oh, God.
> I've done something terrible.
> I've got to put it down. Look at it.
> It is so amazing. That I did it. (C, p. 251)

– and for which there are analogues in *The Magus* – finds its ironic playground in *The French Lieutenant's Woman*:

> Why? Why? Why?
> Blackmail!
> To put him totally in her power! (p. 307)

Charles's hypothesizings in this passage are doomed to remain unanswered, for (as with the neo-gothic of British 1960s novelists) there are mysteries that the book, having urgently invested in, declines to dispel; and this refusal as the book proceeds becomes more resonant and central to its purposes. It is thus a pastiche 1860s sensation novel which turns its later readers into voyeurs of mid-Victorian *mœurs*. It sensational-izes our relations with the received notions of Victorian sexual-ity and flamboyantly plays on the specious temporal distance between the world it invents and the world in which the apparatus of invention is constructed. We look at '1867', that representation of a self-representation (to borrow Derrida's description), through yet another representation which, like the way in which D. H. Lawrence conceived that we now look at the humming-bird ('through the wrong end of the long telescope of time – luckily for us'), domesticates its menace at the same time that it asserts it.

Moreover, the perpetrator of these vulgar conjuring tricks, that procurer of rare *frissons* the Fowlesian narrator himself, unnervingly inserts himself as some Wilkie-Collins-like villain among his own characters (nineteenth-century narrators align themselves more usually in cosy complicity with their gentle readers than with their characters), demonstrating how his prestidigitations occur, soliciting the release of his creatures – characters and readers – from his toils, and foregrounding the related authorial problems of formal foresight and historical hindsight. The middle nineteenth century is symbolically pastoralized, gothicized, elegized, exorcized, and such characteristically mannerist stylization as Prescott Evarts importantly shows – in which an intensification of instability and tension each occur, but without release – is itself a part of the book's subject-matter and hence of its vision.

*

Within the world of styles that it potentiates is a simple action. Charles Smithson, another lonely Fowlesian orphan, is the conventional hero, a somewhat passive leisured gentleman, an amateur of science in general and fossils in particular, intellectually mildly speculative, living with no larger ambition than that of inheriting a baronetcy from his uncle and marrying the daughter of a very rich draper. He is given to the occasional sense of his futility. His fiancée Ernestina is pretty, pert, uninformed, the *Kinder, Kirche und Küche* heroine who aptly and unchallengingly complements his conventionalized masculinity. The late Biedermeier plot their fashion-plate marriage will fulfil is not merely the plot of many of the period's novels but one plot too of nineteenth-century British history, in which land and trade, St James and St Giles, formed so resilient and adaptable a new progressive social hegemony. It is the plot of British social and political evolution, and Charles will give the lie to it.

He meets and gradually falls in love with Sarah Woodruff, the mysterious fallen woman of the title, a social outcast because of the affair she has supposedly had with a French lieutenant. She reminds Charles at different points both of a Parisian *demi-mondaine* he had slept with (p. 64) and also of the Virgin Mary (p. 121). Charles is increasingly torn between Sarah and Ernestina – which is to say, given the uncompromising typology of the male imagination, between Mary and Eve, between a respectably rich virgin and a woman with an alleged past, the woman who is the super-symbol of the story and a classic type of the threat to social normalcy and psychic stability. Like Conchis (and it is relevant here that Fowles wished to make Conchis a woman but found it technically difficult), she is finally unknowable; and her resistance to interpretation is connected, like Conchis's, with her capacity to educate.

The settings for this story of antinomian choice, while acutely and vividly realized, are also appropriately metaphoric. Much of the action takes place in and around the provincial town of Lyme Regis. The town itself, where Charles meets Ernestina, is repressive and parochial, while the neighbouring Undercliff where he meets Sarah is an Edenic a-historical realm of both ethical and botanic 'joyous indiscipline', a place of mythic release. Other locales mirror this duality, so that London, the festive capital of social disparity and sexual hypocrisy, also contains the small room where Charles fails to couple with a second Sarah, a golden-hearted prostitute whose looks, name and condition (abandoned by a soldier-lover) remind him of the original, just as her child also prefigures that of the other Sarah. Exeter, where the social and moral crisis occurs, is strung between its dark, silent cathedral, whose absconded curate points to the absentee God, and its red-light area, 'like most morally dark places . . . full of light and life' (p. 310). Both are liberating enclosures, the latter adjacent to the hotel where

Sarah stays and Charles and she make love, the former eliciting in Charles a new sense of his freedom.

Charles's peripeteia comes, richly decked out in evolutionary metaphor, when his uncle, halfway through the book, unexpectedly marries an 'upper-middle class adventuress', thus – as his wife is young enough to bear children – potentially disinheriting Charles. Tina's father now pressures him into taking an active role in the commercial empire he will inherit, compromising that gentility which living as *rentier* would not have done. The book breeds around Charles's crisis the first of its famous alternative endings, like topological variants thrown out by evolution, not all of which can successfully adapt. This first mutant ending is Charles's sentimental daydream, in which he marries Ernestina, forgets Sarah, has seven children, gets a taste for business and, surrendering to history, prospers. Sam and Mary, the infatuated servants of the subplot, are perfunctorily disposed of. Sarah quietly disappears, while her patroness Mrs Poulteney, the horrid symbol of otiose Grundyism and hypocritical censoriousness, is given an elaborate send-off: 'She fell, flouncing and bannering and ballooning, like a shot crow, down to where her real master waited' (p. 294). This ending is not entirely a token one. The sacrifice of Mrs Poulteney has been twice prefigured (pp. 49, 54) and is later echoed, in each case in exactly these terms, and, according as it does with the modern code of anti-Bowdlerizing, invites our assent. Indeed, the rejection of her values signals the opening out of the book into something very different from what has gone before – into a world whose initial premiss must be the retreat of those forces for which Mrs Poulteney stands. One immediate consequence is that Charles and Sarah have an explosive sexual encounter lasting – the specificity is unignorable in a book so fraught with temporal metaphor – 90 seconds. Immediately after, Charles discovers that, despite having played the role of fallen woman, Sarah was in fact a virgin. She thus combines both halves of the Victorian typology: at exactly the point when she ceases to be a virgin she begins for the first time *to appear to have been one*. Unlike the simply and cloyingly virginal Tina, therefore, Sarah marvellously combines and neutralizes the functions of whore and virgin, a synthesis in its turn pointing to the ways in which she is to appear preternaturally 'modern'. Charles has magically survived the pollution of each taboo only to fall in love.

The rest of the book heightens the mood of erotic quest, as Sarah disappears and Charles hunts for her. It is a hunt that involves his abandoning one by one the hitherto unexamined props to his identity, while the book attempts a comparable formal unclothing. For Fowles as for Sartre, existential truth is always in inverse proportion to social integration; and Sarah, who stands for this truth, stands appropriately also for the subversion of both social and, as we shall see, narrative proprieties. She is an apt magus, and Charles, having already lost his future title and rents, now jilts and hurts Tina, losing his future wife, his good name and social position, and losing also his servant Sam, a defector to exactly that commercial bourgeoisie from which Charles is escaping. Charles becomes a *déraciné*, searching for Sarah in America – that home of the New Woman whose style Sarah is to portend, and where indeed even the fossils are new – but finds her, in one of the book's final and dramatic transgressions, in Bohemian Chelsea, in the house of Dante Gabriel Rossetti. She has a position socially undefined but somehow mandated by the world of art to which she now belongs (she may be Rossetti's model); and she has a child, possibly Charles's.

The Fowlesian narrator has already appeared decisively in his book, aggressively secure and not quite a gentleman in chapter 55, studying Charles in the train and then announcing his intention of showing his neutrality and good faith by presenting the book with two endings. In the first, Charles and Sarah find some kind of future together. The narrator now reappears – as Charles's fortunes decline, his creator's appearances become by inverse proportion flashier and more ambiguous – and puts back his expensive watch one-quarter of an hour. In the second ending, Charles and Sarah part. Despite narrative disclaimers, it is necessarily the more authoritative ending – partly because it is indeed final, partly because it fulfils a deep narrative logic forbidding easy consolation.[30]

*

But the narrative presence – the central source of unifying and complicating pressure within the book – has been throughout ubiquitous. The first chapter establishes relations between narrator and reader, using 'I' four times, 'you' once, and naming no third party among the ghostly assessors it conjures up, though Grogan, the scientifically objective arbiter, makes an unnamed appearance as a telescopic spy. This voice at once establishes readerly consensus, elaborating a historically knowing, far-ranging and richly panoramic documentation of the society and the epoch, of which this simple account of Charles's choice of mate and future is merely one base part. The elaboration involves the deployment of an extraordinary range of subsidiary texts, and the voice is also ceaselessly at work – with a Forsterian wit and energy – monitoring and educating our responses. 'We are not the ones who will finally judge' (p. 46) is a typical early signal about the problematics of securing any privileged overview. In a real sense, this voice is the book's true hero: its heroic work is no less than the simultaneous Faustian reclamation of an imagined historical epoch as well as the exposure of its own compositional resources and historical premises. Its style is a first-person narrative (enclosing and producing the action), which is selectively omniscient, and about which both the extraordinary and imperial extent of its knowingness and talent for ethological typification, and also the singular nature of the limitations it is given to applying to itself, each deserve close attention.

A strong reading of the novel presents it as giving a seductive action of sexual compulsion and moral emancipation, but properly interrupting this (as, notoriously, in chapter 13) with stern and bracing rebukes to our credulity, which as modern readers we know we deserve. We both enjoy the story and are purged of the vulgar imputation of believing it. The story therefore seduces and betrays us exactly as Sarah seduces and then betrays Charles – after which we, like him, face an inconclusive ending and suffer our freedom together. Our story and his thus progressively converge, and when, at the end, he is thrust on to his own resources we are also painfully thrown back on to ours, disappointed perhaps, but freer and better men. The nineteenth and twentieth centuries meet in that guiltless land of existential freedom democratically available to all – writers, readers and novel characters alike:

> My two previous novels were each based on more or less disguised existentialist premises. I want this one to be no exception; and so I am trying to show an existentialist awareness before it was chronologically possible. Kierkegaard was, of course, totally unknown to the British and American Victorians; but it has always seemed to me that the Victorian Age, especially from 1850 on, was highly existentialist in many of its personal dilemmas. One can almost invert the reality and say that Camus and Sartre have been trying to lead us, in their fashion, to a Victorian seriousness of purpose and moral sensitivity. ('Notes', p. 140)

But this passage, like the novel itself, can be used to distil a mythography of decline or homology as much as one of release. Fowles also admiringly notes Thackeray's brilliant technical exercises in the use of 'voice' at the same time that he admits doubts about his own use of omniscient narration, on the grounds of its non-democratic nature. The tactic Fowles actually adopts depends, therefore, not so much on the simple breaking of illusion as on a mannerist intensification of its ambiguities. 'I have disgracefully broken the illusion? No' (p. 86), he announces, after disruptively explaining his theories about the novelist's duty to emancipate his characters from his text. 'My characters still exist, and in a reality no less, or no more, real than the one I have just broken. Fiction is woven into all' (p. 87); and in one interview he suggested that 'this whole fiction-as-illusion thing' only interested him as a way of sharpening the illusion – 'not dispensing with it but learning to live with it' (S, p. 34). If the period of realist ascendancy be figured as Habsburg, then Fowles in this book is a good soldier

Schweik, subverting through an eccentrically literal-minded application the laws of the dispensation under which he must struggle – a much more insidious and effective revolt than a one-man open insurrection. He breaks or conditions illusion by a *reductio ad absurdum* of the principles of authentication, exposing the premises of realism and exciting in the reader a pleasing discomfort comparable to mild epistemological vertigo. As with Schweik, the question of the degree of guile and self-mockery demonstrated is undecidable, and provides its own comedy. The convention he invents, therefore, might also be called super-realism.

So the tone is set in the first chapter by the narrator – exactly like Conchis – twice inviting the Urfe-like reader to corroborate his text. 'I can be put to the test,' he says of his description of the Cobb at Lyme (p. 7), and again, 'I can be put to the proof' (p. 8). Once the verifiability of the text merits such dotty gravity, the omniscience of the narrator can be nearly imperial. This narrative voice has an expertise that is, like its personifications, invasive, omnicompetent, self-gratulatory and ostentatious. In substantiating and colonizing the mid-Victorian world, it exhibits an earnest grasp of the efficacy of epigraphs from sources such as Hardy, Arnold, Clough, Tennyson, Marx, Darwin. It advertises a conspicuous range of intellectual goods and services – always ready for an energetic digression into matters cosmetic, millinery, psychosexual, etymological, political, literary-critical and theological – and shows a keenly fashionable awareness of appropriate socio-historical décor. It has a Peacockian relish for cultural free enterprise, quirk and quiddity, and is much given to a historical transaction in which it explains each epoch to its neighbour.

The degree of penetration is indeed striking. 'Charles called himself a Darwinist, and yet he had not really understood Darwin. But then, nor had Darwin' (p. 47). The voice, employing a Forsterian 'bounce', proudly gives a twentieth-century overview in which the full relativizing consequences of Darwinism now become apparent. Again, in chapter 35, a long but crucial disquisition on Victorian sexuality, Hardy's thwarted affair with his cousin Tryphena, its tension between repression and release 'energises and *explains* one of the age's greatest writers' (p. 236; my italics). This tension, which is also that between (male) explanation and (female) secrecy, is the central funding antinomy of the book. The narrator hypothesizes that the Victorians 'experienced a much keener, because less frequent sexual pleasure than we do' and aptly points out that our liberation from censorship is also an impoverishment:

> by transferring to the public imagination what they left to the private, we are the more Victorian – in the derogatory sense of the word – century, since we have, in destroying much of the mystery, the difficulty, the aura of the forbidden, destroyed also a great deal of the pleasure. (p. 234)

Frustration is the mother of imagination, and this tension energizes Fowles's fiction as much as Hardy's.[31] It necessarily affects the narrative voice and its range of effects. Omniscience is not baffled by Sam's erotic fantasies (which concern collars), and, though it has an explicit sexual politics of its own, nor does even the subconscious of Mrs Poulteney (the Jungian Terrible Mother) inhibit it: the goings-on on Ware Commons had become 'the objective correlative of all that went on in her own subconscious' (p. 83). What does occasion its scrupulous seizing-up and public compunction, promoting the hectic caesura of chapter 13, is the attempt to see Sarah intrinsically instead of contextually. 'Who is Sarah? Out of what shadows does she come?' ends chapter 12; and it is this question that provokes the flamboyant agnosticism of chapter 13 beginning 'I do not know'. Any suspicion that this is fortuitous must be dispelled by the recurrence of this note on p. 243: 'and I no more intend to find out what was going on in her mind . . . than I did on that other occasion'. Selective omniscience is governed in part by the *anima*. Mrs Poulteney is absolutely knowable, down to her subconscious; Charles knowable both contextually and intrinsically (though he has the limited freedom to go into the dairy without authorial permission). But Sarah is a subjectivity wholly unknowable, and – to some degree echoed

70

by her surrogate Mary in this respect – the object of a quest which is as explicitly that of the narrative voice as it is that of Charles. All characters may be ideally autonomous; but some are more autonomous than others.

*

It is the local and sustained treatment of temporal metaphor which so distinguishes this singular novel and which creates an enabling context out of which the more operatic metalepses are generated. These local plays on narrative decorum are original and deeply paradoxical. The author-as-stage-manager after all occurs in Thackeray. Dickens may not have intended his two alternative endings to *Great Expectations* to coexist in one volume, but James Antony Froude's *The Lieutenant's Daughter*, an 1847 novella with startling similarities to Fowles's own (but which he had not read), certainly leaves the choice of endings to the reader. Emily Brontë's *Wuthering Heights* (1847) openly presents two versions of the same story, and a footnote to Hardy's *The Return of the Native* (1878) offers an unhappy ending to those with 'an austere artistic code'. And it was Anthony Trollope (as James showed in *The House of Fiction*), that most 'inert' of Victorian realists, who habitually took 'a suicidal satisfaction in reminding the reader that the story he was telling was only, after all, make-believe'.[32] Chapter 17 of *Adam Bede* and all of *Northanger Abbey* point to those metaleptic effects that Gérard Genette in *Narrative Discourse* has shown are the commonplaces of narrative in most periods, not excluding the Victorian. What distinguishes the fertility and formal resource of the Victorian novel from contemporary experiment is that the former could be said to be the careless product of radical epistemological and aesthetic confidence, while the latter is the child often of a neo-Platonic formal desperation.

Thus Sarah's functional unknowability enables her immunity to the values of the worlds of either confidence or desperation, and she develops from Foucault's sexual hysteric into an a-historic figure. Early in the book she reads to Mrs Poulteney and 'did not create in her voice . . . an unconscious alienation

71

effect of the Brechtian kind . . . but the very contrary: she spoke directly of the sufferings of Christ . . . *as if there were no time in history*' (p. 54; my italics). This important passage, apart from making a parallel between Sarah and Christ, also evinces a nostalgia for direct speech and for the world indemnified against change which her voice enshrines. Once there is time in history, it might conversely be observed, alienation effects in narrative are possible if not enjoined. The anachronistic conjunction of Mrs Poulteney and Brecht is exactly one such effect, and one of a kind in which the book abounds. It has been suggested that they provide a Barthesian *effet du réel*, co-opting the fictional world into the world of history and providing it with veristic guarantees. But they also provide a small sensational *frisson*, dependent on the ontological surprise and menace they (e.g. Brecht and Mrs Poulteney) offer one another. A neo-gothic collision occurs between a ghostly imagined fictive past and a phantom historical present in which, while history 'validates' the novel by making it an enclave of itself, the novel also makes of history a species of client-text subserving its own needs. These conjunctions themselves produce a species of alienation effect – albeit like Brecht's own devices, not always strictly Brechtian ones, but reminiscent perhaps of a double exposure on a photograph. Our experience of local temporal flow in the novel is defamiliarized and experienced as disjunction and conjunction.

While some such effects are anxiously tonal – as when we are reminded that Sam's role playing is *ante* Stanislavski (p. 285) – others are more deliberate provocations – as when, for example, Charles, after completing his lovemaking with Sarah, is described as like a city struck out of a quiet sky by an atom bomb (p. 305), or we are assured that Ernestina died on the day that Hitler invaded Poland (p. 29), or that the Gestapo would have found a place for Mrs Poulteney (p. 23). Many of the effects play on the gap between historical explanation and secrecy, with the folly of narrative wisdom itself on display. Thus the reason that Mrs Poulteney did not have books about her was not because she was an early forerunner of the 'egregious McLuhan' (p. 37); Charles knew nothing of Marx, the 'beavered German Jew quietly working, . . . that very afternoon in the British Museum library; and whose work in those sombre walls was to bear such bright red fruit' (p. 16). Charles's ignorance of Marx, like Darwin's of Darwin, is rebuked by a doubly omniscient hindsight, which both plots his movements *vis-à-vis* a historical figure and displays its knowledge of period slang ('beaver' = beard).

The interpenetration of fictive past and historical present is persistently, teasingly assured. Mary's great-great-granddaughter is a famous English film actress; the narrator now possesses a Toby jug bought by Sarah; a cottage on Ware Commons now belongs to a fashionable London architect. The deep necessary illogic of Fowles's chosen narrative mode is displayed in such a way that a variety of readings and interpretations are always possible. There is, as I have suggested, an aprioristic distribution of degrees of freedom among the characters of the book, with only Charles exemplarily fully educable.

Charles moves between the pole of unfreedom represented by the public and fixed subjection of Mrs Poulteney to historical values on the one hand, and the pole of freedom, suggested by the secret but equally fixed 'autonomy' of Sarah, on the other. But such varieties of historical detachment are themselves often produced out of an odd and paradoxical sense of the ways in which a fiction can encode a moral style in historical flow. The stigmata of salvation can most often be recognized by the degree to which characters are born into or adopt the style of their epoch. When we are told of Sarah's face that 'it was certainly not a beautiful face by any period's standard or taste' and moreover that she was 'totally indifferent to fashion', the narrative tone is as plainly disingenuous as when it tells us 'Mary's face was not, *I'm afraid*, the face for 1867' (my italics); each is secretly, differently indemnified against jejune local values – ethical as much as aesthetic – of that or other periods. In precise contrast, poor Ernestina, dismissible because wholly explicable, has 'exactly the right face for her age, that is small-chinned, oval, delicate as a violet'. Resistance to the bad faith of the epoch need not depend on prolepsis. It can oddly rely on preservation. The camphor Mrs Poulteney carries on her person as a protection against cholera gives out an odour of mothballs, which points to the way her values too belong to the museum of time; but Grogan's Augustanism, or Aunt Tranter's early Victorian furniture, could be said to stand for a vivification of the past. So when Ernestina's vulgar daydream about marrying Charles and taking over the old house he will inherit involves 'a comprehensive replacement of all those absurd scrolly chairs (Carolean and almost priceless), gloomy cupboards (Tudor), moth-eaten tapestries (Gobelins) and dull paintings (including two Claudes and a Tintoretto) that did not meet her approval', it is clear which way the compositional resource of sympathy is being pressed, and how much weight a merely modish modernity is to carry. Her modernity is of a kind that causes her to giggle at a *Punch* cartoon showing a female Cabinet minister (p. 101) – thus as conspicuously missing one incumbent social revolution, just as Charles, mis-reading the signs of emancipation in his servant Sam's struggle with his accent, misses another (p. 41).

Perhaps the complexity of anachronistic effect that the book can produce is best shown in an early passage in which Sam prepares to shave Charles:

> Sam stood stropping his razor, and steam rose invitingly, with a kind of Proustian richness of evocation – so many happy days, so much assurance of position, order, calm, civilisation, out of the copper jug he had brought with him. (p. 38)

The conjunction of Sam and Proust is nostalgic in a perplexing way. The mood could be described as one of anticipatory nostalgia, or as creating a prospective retrospect. Since Proust is an early twentieth-century seeker after a late nineteenth-century past, used here as a symbol of the sensual plenitude of memory in the nineteenth century, but within a text which reminds us that it is produced from the mid-twentieth, the effect is a startling mixture of prospect and retrospect, each framed within our own retrospect so that the scene is co-temporal with its own tranquil imagined future (to itself), past (to us) re-enactment. The effects of historical homology, de-cline and release are each differently and not always singly solicited.

Charles's story is associated with his hobby of palaeontology and set against the plot of evolution. Until Freeman attempts to hector the now perhaps disinherited Charles into commerce, the pervasive Hardyesque metaphor of evolution works, albeit with much irony, on his side. He notes that 'inexorable laws very conveniently arranged themselves for the survival of the fittest and best, *exempli gratia* Charles Smithson' (p. 47; see also pp. 142, 144), in testimony to which he has shot one of the last great bustards on Salisbury Plain and contributed to the extinction of an 'inferior' species. In keeping with this metaphor, encounters between Mrs Poulteney and Lady Cot-ton are, to the narrator, essentially 'clashes between Bronto-sauri' (p. 88), and Ernestina courts Charles by describing the competing claims of other women as 'early Cretaceous'. When Freeman argues with Charles about the latter's going into business, he uses the argument that a species must change in order to survive (p. 250). Immediately after this interview, Charles pictures the 'gentleman' as an obsolescent species like the bustard, a 'living fossil' (p. 253). Charles becomes that quintessentially Fowlesian hero, 'a man struggling to overcome history' (p. 257), standing in fact against the vast pressures of the evolutionary plot itself.

The release he seeks from unremitting determinism is given in the book's most audacious anachronism, a mysterious yield-ing of the unceasing sequentiality of the plot of history itself to the authentic action of the will, which is to say to the felt choice of freedom. Deserted by evolution, he is rescued by existential-ism. Though the Victorians do not have 'the lessons of existen-tialist philosophy at [their] disposal' (p. 63) and, later, 'were not the people for existentialist moments, but for chains of cause and effect' (p. 215), the book evolves a theology much like that of Renaissance humanism about the salvation of the Virtuous Pagan. Just as the countless generations of good men born before Christ were to have the benefit of the afterlife, even though they were deprived of the new eschatological wisdom, so Charles, though 'he had not the benefit of existentialist terminology' (p. 296), can still find grace. He has two important epiphanies from which he is to intuit his means of egress.

> In a vivid insight, a flash of black lightning, he saw that all life was parallel: that evolution was not vertical, ascending to a perfection, but horizontal. Time was the great fallacy; exitence was without history, was always now, was always being caught in the same fiendish machine. (p. 179)

This perception, aptly engendered soon after his worldly disinheritance, promises a privileged mode of insight for him and, by implication, for his epoch. It is echoed when, dispossessing himself further, he sets out for that assignation with Sarah in which the real state of his feelings will become apparent to him and when 'the moment overcame the age' (p. 217). It is a morning of intense lyrical beauty in which he is confronted by the 'universal parity of existence' (p. 208). After his encounter with the prostitute pseudo-Sarah, he again 'had a far more profound and genuine intuition of the great illusion about time, which is that its reality is like a road . . . instead of the truth: that time is a room, a now so close to us that we regularly fail to see it' (p. 278). The historical road of evolutionary lore gives way to the room of existentialist lore, in which every moment presents a mythic choice and the enclosure opens to disclose freedom.

*

The creative and 'plebeian pleasures of anachronism' are used in *The French Lieutenant's Woman* with some adroitness. The Fowlesian search for personal authenticity and fullness occurs within a text insistently and stagily boastful about its own historically bound inauthenticity and incompleteness. The drama of the narrative voice, alternately monarch and puppet, magisterial and duplicitous, echoes the drama of the protagonist, struggling comparably to perceive himself as one agent within a world of subjectivities. The text is equally caught between the need to authenticate itself and the need to punish and denounce its old obligation towards history; it aspires, with some success, to renegotiate the mandate of realism.

5

'THE EBONY TOWER'

It was a forest setting again, but with a central clearing, much more peopled than usual, less of the sub-aqueous feeling, under a first-class blue, almost a black, that managed to suggest both night and day, both heat and storm, a looming threat over the human component. ('The Ebony Tower')

The French Lieutenant's Woman could be said to examine the literary tradition in which Fowles's storytelling technique and narrative drive have one origin. *The Ebony Tower* (1974) goes back further to examine those roots, not in the age of classic realism, but in the landscape of those romances in which Fowles, with a brave partiality, locates the birth of fiction itself: the landscape of the Celtic romances of the early Middle Ages, with their mysterious conflation of passion and a legalistic sense of duty. This volume contains four stories and a translation of Marie de France's 'Eliduc'. In an introduction to this translation Fowles argues that 'we owe the very essence of what we have meant by the fictional, the novel and its children, to this strange Northern invasion of the medieval mind' (p. 120). The title story 'The Ebony Tower' is set in Brittany and makes reference to 'Eliduc'. The other three stories, one set in central France, play with narrative convention as we inherit it, dealing variously with the pathos or comedy of disappearing texts and disappearing selves. Fowles originally intended the title 'Variations' for the collection, and indeed they provide permutations both on one another and on the materials addressed in the novels.

The title story, which is the most successful of the collection, returns to the themes of *The Magus*: 'In a way I wanted to demystify *The Magus* which I think was altogether too full of mystery. This is a kind of realistic version of *The Magus*' (R). Indeed, at one point the protagonist David Williams sees one of the girls in this story reading *The Magus* and thinks, with an appropriate irony, 'He guessed at astrology, she would be into all that nonsense' (p. 65). Like *The Magus*, the story concerns an initiation through sexual loss; unlike Urfe, whose phil-andering life-mood is the symptom of an inner decay, David Williams was a 'crypto-husband' even before he contentedly married: if Urfe is coerced into imagining sexual loyalty for the first time, it is sexual disloyalty that is presented as Williams's redemption. Where *The Magus* was persistently concerned at a subtextual level with art (and Urfe was a failed artist, Conchis a quasi-artist), it is of the first importance that Williams and Breasley, the postulant and magus of 'The Ebony Tower', are practitioners: Breasley an artist of high repute, Williams wed-ded to safety and the second-rate in his art as, by implication, in his marriage. It is an immensely concentrated story which distils an existential ordeal and love-triangle; the action takes place against a debate about the destiny of art in our century which – though the art in question is visual rather than narrative – conditions the story's outcome. Williams's moment of truth, moreover, is situated (as we shall see) at a point of strain in relation to the artistic wisdom that prompts it.

David Williams is a competent abstract painter whose work tamely flatters current artistic fashion; it goes well in certain domestic interiors. He is comfortably married to a successful illustrator of children's books; they live in London, a contented couple. He is commissioned to edit a book on Henry Breasley, a great renegade artist living in self-imposed exile in Brittany, at Coetminais, the 'Forest of the Monks'. The story opens with Williams's aesthetic pleasure at the autumn landscape observed on his journey from Cherbourg. Coetminais turns out to be an old and unassuming manor set in the remains of an ancient forest. He enters the lost domain – another Fowlesian land of lost content – and meets Breasley's two girl compan-ions, nicknamed the Mouse and the Freak. Their ménage is an unconventional one. There is an ambiguity about whether the ministrations of the girls are sexual as well as domestic.

Williams first views the girls naked; at a later stage, he swims with them naked. Coetminais partakes, in the typical discontinuity of romance, of the character of a pre-socialized and a-historical womb, a place from which the past can transmit its special understanding to the future.

Though Coetminais stands in some sense outside local social conventions, it is very much to the point that it is not outside artistic convention. The first night at supper, Breasley, an old-fashioned and half-articulate Bohemian maverick, launches an attack on the values he sees as underpinning both Williams's art and the artistic establishment of the day. The modern is, as he sees it, the age of institutionalized amnesia, in which there is no discernible tradition except that of, in Ortega's phrase, 'the dehumanization of art', a reaction to the sense of historical crisis. His own painting is eclectic and represents 'an improbable marriage of Samuel Palmer and Chagall' (p. 18). It is often described as 'Celtic', and in it there is a recurrence, as in the story itself, of 'the forest motif, the enigmatic figures and confrontations' (p. 19). It owes something to Pisanello's Arthurian paintings and stands in a relation of ironic homage to the art of the past.

One of the somewhat Pre-Raphaelite series of paintings on which he is currently engaged – the Coetminais series – shows a blue-black colour which is a 'looming threat over the human component' (p. 29). His charge against contemporary art is that this looming threat, which he sees as the threat of abstraction as against empathy, has been allowed an unconsidered and absolute victory. Williams, who is himself an abstract painter with an admiration for Braque (a painter represented in Breasley's collection), is attacked, with some scatological resource, as a eunuch, a bum-boy; Picasso is Pick-arse. He attempts to defend himself on the grounds that these are ancient quarrels and can be contained by an intelligent pluralism, a toleration of all styles. For Breasley, however, this is liberal cant. Abstraction depends upon a totalitarian aesthetics; it represents the triumph of cold technique over matter, a surrender of feeling to scientific rationality and organization. It is the great betrayal, a flight from human and social responsibility. 'The only answer to fascism is the human fact' (p. 50), a fact most evident in its physical and sexual aspect. He names this betrayal 'the ebony tower', a corruption of the ivory tower of late Romanticism which relegates art to a state of solitary confinement in which, obscurantist, it can commune only with a tiny audience of client-intellectuals: it is a version of the 'enclosure' itself, but become entirely and irresponsibly self-purposive.

After this ordeal-by-jeremiad, the following day Williams faces ordeals of a new kind. Diana, nicknamed the Mouse by Breasley as a private sexual joke, explains Breasley to Williams. Her mediations bring her and Williams closer. She has been described by Breasley as a Lizzie Siddall, and first struck Williams as 'nineteenth-century': as always with Fowles's temp-tresses – and she is perhaps the best realized of them all – there is something uncontemporary about her. She combines the functions of Sarah and Lily: a lost yet serious girl whose special quality is carefully distinguished from the more extravagant and evident appeal of her vamp-like friend the Freak, with her complementarily dyed head and pubic hair. She herself finds the 'faintly mythic and timeless' quality of Coetminais both constituting and threatening, and it is a quality in which she is deeply implicated. Breasley has proposed marriage to her and, hurt by her relationships with younger men, she is tempted by both his compassion and his authority, and also divided by her desire as an artist herself to be out in the world and subject to its fearful anarchy.

The speed with which both the estate and Diana have David equally in thrall is masterfully done. The magic of Coetminais is explicitly connected with Celtic romance, and Breasley's genius has been 'to take an old need to escape from the city, for a mysterious remoteness, and to see its ancient solution, the Celtic green source, was still viable' (p. 77). In this world of yearning, of the suggestive 'nonsense' of the romances, the disorientations of *The Magus* are compressed into a very short span. David is deeply stirred by Diana and finds himself assigned the role of possible knight-errant, rescuing her from her predicament. When the logic of their mutual feeling requires him to renounce the safety of his marriage and certainties of his future and elope with her, he hesitates and loses her: her bedroom door is locked against him. This loss of nerve is presented as a failure of his moral being, connected to the mediocrity of his art. He compares himself unfavourably to Breasley, who has the artistically productive temperament – so the story romantically asserts – for 'excess and ruthless egocentricity' (p. 113). Breasley stands up bravely to the existential imperative constantly to recast the self, and, like some Lawrentian hero, is still, as an old man, in touch with the grand and amoral physical wisdom of the body. Against Breasley's ruthless opportunism, David's renunciation of the body in his art is supposedly an aspect of the physical timidity he shows with Diana.

David is condemned, he comes to see, to be 'a decent man and eternal also-ran' (p. 113). The programmatic rootlessness of post-war art claims him at the same time that he realizes that his own cultural roots – in the wife who meets him in the ending's present tense – have circumscribed him. Breasley may stand for the courageous acceptance of filiation with artistic tradition in an age whose reflexes are modishly iconoclastic. He may stand against contemporary historical special pleading and self-pity for the bitter heroism of artistic *memory*. But the life-mood for which David is criticized is one in which he himself remembers his obligations to historical fact in the form of his marriage: the *cultural* amnesia that his desertion of his wife would have presented is by contrast presented as honorific. The novella is only partly self-conscious about this.

The source of mood, theme and setting in 'The Ebony Tower' had been that medieval romance of which 'Eliduc' is one example (p. 119), and Breasley has admiringly referred to 'Eliduc', which deals explicitly with this conflict between sexual passion and duty. William's predecessor Eliduc is a medieval knight who makes Williams's journey in reverse, travelling from Brittany to England, after swearing fidelity to the wife he leaves behind. In England he is accepted into the service of a king for whom he fights and with whose daughter he falls passionately in love, as does she with him. When the Breton king recalls him, he abducts and returns with this girl, but without explaining his circumstances to her; on the voyage home she learns that he has a wife and collapses as if dead. He lays her body before the altar of a disused chapel and returns to his wife, with whom he perfunctorily tries to revive the life of marital obligation. His thoughts are with the girl in the chapel, which he daily visits. His wife learns of these pilgrimages and, discovering the girl herself, weeps for all three of them. She sees a weasel reviving its dead mate by placing a red forest flower in its mouth and succeeds in reviving the girl with the same flower. She makes a gift of the girl and her husband to one another, renouncing the world herself and becoming a nun. Eliduc and his new love live together in perfect harmony until, all passion spent in old age, they too give up the world. Eliduc's two wives end up comforting one another in the convent, while he too loves God. All die peacefully.

The story as Fowles presents it speaks for the magical reconciliation of love in its passionate, divine and social guises. The agent of miraculous truce is the red flower known to the weasel, and it too plays a part in 'The Ebony Tower' when David, a third of the way between Diana, whom he has left at Coetminais, and his wife in Paris, runs over a weasel and sees that 'a trickle of blood, like a red flower, had spilt from the gaping mouth' (p. 108). His choice, unlike Eliduc's, is evidently an irremediable one.

At the end of 'The Ebony Tower' the narrative voice comments that David 'surrenders to what is left: to abstraction'. 'I survived,' he tells his wife. But the conflict between David and Breasley is not schematic and contains paradoxes. David himself, though committed to abstraction, is 'tending towards nature and away from . . . high artifice' (p. 21); though Breasley attacks Braque, he also venerates him and owns one of his paintings; though he attacks Hitler, he wears a Hitlerite moustache; though he apparently speaks against the abdication of art from its moral and humane function, the lesson he teaches

David is that 'art is fundamentally immoral' (p. 113); moreover, Coetminais curiously mirrors the world in that David, who is married to an ex-art student, is also tempted by an ex-art student in Diana. Breasley speaks with an incoherent passion of the responsibility of art toward the human, and the debate he addresses is one in which mimesis or representation in art is a matter to be either denounced or defended. Yet the most sombre in the Coetminais series on which he is working is inspired by Foxe's *Book of Martyrs* and shows 'a wood of hanged figures and of living ones who seemed as if they wished they were hanged' (p. 80), as though elegizing, perhaps, the failure of his own artistic vision to differentiate clearly a living human element. And though he defends the narrative, anecdotal and literary dimensions of painting, which constitute also that representational function, his best work refines these into compositional devices (p. 31).

The complexities of the argument, as the story as a whole enacts them, are reflected in its techniques. Since the action is seen by a painter, the scenes of the story, as Mills shows, tend to arrange themselves around paintings[33] – Manet, Chardin, de la Tour, Pisanello. Just as these painters necessarily and variously conventionalized their perception of nature, so the elaboration of the painterly analogy itself points to that conventionalization upon which all narrative also depends. The putative common origin that the story creates – in the magically attended natural scenes of Pisanello, with their chivalrous saints – is in courtly romance, with its twin pulls of sexual passion and social duty, of attention to both sacred and profane. 'The Ebony Tower' handles these rival and complementary claims, of abstraction and empathy, romance and realism, the demands of the magical enclosure and the requirements of that world outside it which the enclosure predicates, with a command and subtlety not always apparent in *The Magus*, whose problems it also recapitulates.

*

The insecure tenure of the self in relation to the text is in a sense Fowles's chosen problematic in these stories. For Breasley the disappearing text of past art itself sanctifies a particular arena of moral and aesthetic choice in the present life of the artist. 'Poor Koko' deals with another kind of disappearing text. As 'The Enigma' plays with the convention of the detective story, so this tale – like *The Collector*, which it also resembles thematically – uses for its very different ends the convention of the thriller. The narrator, a slightly precious old *littérateur* belonging to a world that is being demolished around him, is nearing the end of a lifetime's ambition: the writing of a critical biography of Thomas Love Peacock (a favourite author of Fowles, too). He is a short and physically weak man, and his most successful potboiler to date is 'The Dwarf in Literature'. He takes his Peacock notes and manuscripts to a remote North Dorset cottage where, late at night, he hears a burglar at work. He and the burglar confront one another and fail – like Clegg and Miranda, and like the family who own the cottage and are themselves divided by generation – to come to any understanding of one another. The young man is socially resentful, perceives himself as a judicious agent in a world corrupted by property, enjoys reading Joseph Conrad, but is (in the older man's terms) only semi-articulate. He talks, indeed, a strange classless discourse: 'You're just saying words, man' (p. 161). He believes that fine art should be publicly available in museums, knows a good deal about antiques and never takes the most valuable objects, which might be traceable, but cunningly stages his thefts so that they appear to be the work of an amateur. He thus picks unremarkable but still profitable goods. A counter-cultural burglar, he sees himself as carefully eschewing the limitless greed that has spoilt society as a whole.

The burglar ties up and gags the narrator, showing considerable care and even tenderness. He then takes the Peacock manuscript and systematically burns it in front of his eyes. The story so far is a preamble to a meditation by the narrator on the meaning of this crisis – a meditation which fails to elicit any tidy conclusion, but which points to a failure of transmission. It is not merely that the two have failed to communicate, but that the narrator was in possession of a cultural wealth that had not been made properly available to the burglar. The narrator sees their conversation as concealing a plea on the burglar's part for this secret wisdom, and the act of biblioclasm is then a revenge on the culture of literacy from which he has been unfairly excluded. The epigraph is a monitory one, appropriately enough in a dead language (Cornish). 'Too long a tongue, too short a hand; but tongueless man has lost his land': a sad testimony to the primacy of language in conserving national culture. The title 'Poor Koko' refers to the Japanese word meaning correct filial behaviour, the proper attitude of son to father. The story, therefore, like 'The Ebony Tower', refers to the disruption of the line of artistic and cultural filiation, and speaks of the ways in which the authority of the text itself authenticates the reading self, or fails to do so.

*

Fowles has paid his respects to the detective tale elsewhere, and 'The Enigma', which after 'The Ebony Tower' is one of the collection's most successful stories, is also an ironic tribute to the genre. Its disappearing protagonist John Marcus Fielding, successful lawyer, country squire, member of parliament and quintessential public man, stands in a precisely obverse relation to Breasley. Fowles has elsewhere distinguished the public British face of jingoism and cant from the private English search for justice in the greenwood; it is a thesis much elaborated in *Daniel Martin* too. The figure of Robin Hood the just outlaw, living in touch with an ancient forest wisdom, comes to stand for all that Fowles finds enduring and valuable in the English soul, as well as illuminating English hypocrisy: 'in this habitual disappearance into the metaphorical greenwoods, this retreat behind the mask of our ability to simulate agreement when we disagree, to smile when we hate, to say the exact opposite of what we mean' ('On Being English'). 'Robin Hoodism' for Fowles stands for the English genius for protecting the substantial self in an age that seeks to superannuate it elsewhere: a talent for empiricism and individualism. The English self in inhospitable ages (like the present) goes into hiding, and the English are expert practitioners of privacy, concealment

86

and duplicity. Hence those heroic exiled Englishmen-in-disguise, Conchis and Breasley, outliving a bad time in exile but distilling some special authenticity in their green enclosures.

'The Enigma' utilizes the detective tale in the service of much grander literary effects. The story of the disappearance of a public man, it begins with the statistical evidence about disappearances. Its opening is a pastiche of a classic type of detective tale, of which Daphne du Maurier's 'No Motive' would be a representative example. In this story the tough, sentimental, omnicompetent cop uncovers the complete and formerly secret biography of a missing self, and, having disclosed the ghostly dossier to us, withholds it from the family it would hurt. The detective tale is in this sense one paradigm of fiction, presenting a mystery in a closed world of signs so constructed as to permit the illusion of a total decoding. The complete solution of the disorders of the plot and the dissolution of its enigmas in the face of the urge to omniscience are each ironized by Fowles, who uses the genre in pursuit again of the insight that is sprung when the conventions are refused the closure they seek. Realism, it seems, can no longer be policed. 'The Enigma' is in this sense a comic tale whose sustained documentary elaboration of what is known of Fielding's public life (much) and what can be surmised of his intrinsic nature (little) is a bait for the reader and a preparation for instructive disappointment. 'Then if our story disobeys the unreal literary rules, that might mean it's actually truer to life?' (p. 236) Isabel, who was Fielding's son's girlfriend, asks the middle-class detective Jennings.

The increasing collaboration of Isabel and Jennings provides the story with its momentum and also such closure as it achieves. Their mutual researches produce a picture of sorts. Fielding wished to be both a rich man on the grab and a pillar of the community, squaring private opportunism and public conscience. Like his son Peter, he may have felt the strain of reconciling public and private modes of being and may have been 'two different people' (pp. 217, 231). Isabel, another existential heroine who 'lived in the present' (p. 222) and who, unlike the Fieldings, knows how to 'be herself' (p. 232), is an apprentice novelist who theorizes that everything to do with the Fieldings, including Jennings and herself, is in a novel: 'Nothing is real. All is fiction.' Indemnified against verification, she suggests that she and Fielding may have met, and possibly in the British Museum Reading Room, that house of fiction itself – where he was last known to have gone. It would have been the quintessential Fowlesian tryst, hollow man confronting authentic woman. Fielding, a minor character in a bad book, had kept all his press cuttings, that text of the public persona within which he may have felt his inner self to be totally subsumed. His absconding, then, becomes another idealist levitation out of a determining public plot, akin to God's absconding, or to the Sheriff of Nottingham himself going out of bounds, back into that Sherwood Forest where he can feel he has at last created a legend worthy of the part of his being he had formerly suppressed. 'The one thing people never forget is the unsolved' (p. 239), as Isabel puts it. As for the detective, he is conventionally the agent of protection of middle-class accumulation, within which the substantial self itself might be said to be the ultimately sanctified property value. But Jennings is an unusual and distinctive detective, and the narrative voice finally brings him and Isabel together in what is, for Fowles, a rare moment of consummated love and an adequate conclusion in itself. 'The tender pragmatisms of flesh have poetries no enigma, human or divine, can diminish or demean – indeed, it can only cause them and walk out' (p. 244). The absconding of the Fowlesian narrator, like that of the authoritarian God, and of the worldly Fielding, is done with unusual delicacy.

*

In 'The Cloud', the most uneven and ambitious of the stories, the disappearing self is that of Catherine, a bereaved girl on holiday with a party of bourgeois English in central France. The class to which it is made clear she belongs is the one in whose interests not merely the police work, but for whom much fiction ('an adamantly bourgeois form', ZB, p. 124) has been a parish magazine. One characteristic verbal usage of this class is the indirect 'one', which conceals the universalizing of a local set of values. The narrative voice employs this Virginia-Woolf-like 'one' in much the way she used it, in order that the disembodied sensitive supra-consciousness of the tale should mediate between the points of view of its characters, yet conceal its own movements while so employed. If 'The Enigma' provokes and frustrates expectation, 'The Cloud' might be said to embarrass it. It is consistently arch about its conventionality. 'So many things clashed, or were not as might have been expected. If one had been there, of course' (p. 248); 'One (blessed sanctuary) could see Catherine trying to make an effort' (p. 255).

Efforts to include and cheer Catherine are made by her sharper and more complete sister Bel, by Bel's novelist husband Paul, by various of their children, and finally by Paul's irrevocably meretricious friend Peter, a television producer who, with her encouragement, sodomizes her. Catherine emerges as a mixture of Sarah in *The French Lieutenant's Woman*, foreseeing and inviting her defilement, and possibly, like one of Muriel Spark's characters, prescient too about her own death.

6

'DANIEL MARTIN'

> Beyond the specific myth of each novel, the novelist longs to
> be possessed by the continuous underlying myth he enter-
> tains of himself . . . ('Hardy and the Hag')

Among the decently redeemable characters in 'The Cloud' is
the novelist Paul, ox-like, nautically bearded, a man with 'sales
if not name' (p. 263) and with an 'awful Russian monk' within
him that prompts him to expound 'grand cultural rhubarb'
even while his sister-in-law undergoes her crisis. This impotent
Fowlesian novelist, an arrogant cultural imperialist, right-
thinking (unlike his depraved friend Peter) but lacking healing
power, and incarnated once more within his own work, seems
deliberately to invite some awkward questions about narrative
self-government.

Constance Hieatt, in a scholarly essay on 'Eliduc', notes both
how biased and partial is Fowles's translation from Old
French, and also how easily it subserves male fantasy. Eliduc in
the original, Hieatt argues, is a morally dark figure, numbering
murder and betrayal among his misdeeds, and the inhuman
generosity of his wife requires to be read less as a pastoral
collusion with 'romantic love' than as a bitter feminine bowing
to masculine *force majeure*: 'Fowles is almost exclusively
concerned with the problems of men, even when he devotes a
major part of the narrative to looking at a woman's point of
view.'[34]

I should like to return here to the problem of the sexual
politics of Fowles's fiction. In his personal note to 'Eliduc'
midway through 'The Ebony Tower', Fowles suggests that
'*amour courtois* was a desperately needed attempt to bring

more civilisation (more female intelligence) into a brutal society' (p. 124). He refers, indeed, to the system of courtly love as a 'real life code'. This is a curious description. The question of the degree to which courtly love was a social and to what degree a literary code, a useful fiction or piece of instant nostalgia, is a delicate one.[35] To most commentators there is a necessary and direct connection between a social system in which women were sold and forced into marriage and a *literary* code in which they appeared as demi-goddesses. The feudalization of love, which has thus far been a permanent feature of Fowles's fiction, rests uneasily on this paradox: that the sexual idealization of women has acted as the destructive condition under which their repression could continue unabated. As Mill in *On the Subjection of Women* put it, 'we are perpetually being told that women are better than men by those who are totally opposed to treating them as if they were as good.'[36] This text of Mill's is, of course, one that *The French Lieutenant's Woman* mentions approvingly. Outside his fiction Fowles has consistently argued for two opposed but related principles. Feminism is necessary, but for men in particular, since much current sickness 'arises from the selfish tyranny of the male'; 'all progressive philosophies are feminist', and all innovatory periods in history – like the Renaissance or the modern period – are 'Eve societies' (*A*, p. 166). Great revolutionary periods are epochs of female domination because 'women are freer creatures than men' (UEA).

This makes for an oddly complacent kind of feminism. 'It always worries me when I see the feminine principle itself being attacked by women,' he has understandably said, and he has deplored the denial by feminists of 'the extraordinary half-maternal, half-mysterious aspect of women' (*JML*, p. 190). For Fowles the *ewig Weibliche* repeatedly subserves the male by modifying, civilizing, forgiving and educating the stupefying power of masculine brutality and egoism, and women tend to appear in his romances as tutors, muses, sirens, nannies and gnomic trustees of the mysteriousness of existence, as well as Persecuted Maidens and *princesses lointaines*. Breasley is one

91

paradigm of a man who needs women around him because of 'Sense of timing. Bleeding and all that' (*ET*, p. 29). Once women in Fowles's work perilously focus the action themselves and try to escape these roles, the narrative generally has ways of disposing of them. Fowles has thus also identified the birth of fiction with the twelfth-century discovery of, among other things, '*Amor*' (*ET*, p. 120) – an identification that will not bear much scrutiny. Classical romances such as the *Satyricon*, *The Golden Ass* and *Daphnis and Chloe* deal in a spirit of picaresque and amoral cheerfulness with the full variety of human sexuality. The puritanization and related romanticization of heterosexual love in the early Middle Ages, associated with Mariolatry, does, however, clearly make for a different kind of disposition of erotic frustration and release in fiction, one in which Fowles's work has a very large vested interest. He has shown a predilection for those contexts in which courtly love has some purchase: the nineteenth century in *The French Lieutenant's Woman* in which – unlike the twelfth century of 'Eliduc' – it achieved its domestic and bourgeois apotheosis; the a-historical domains of *The Magus* and 'The Ebony Tower'.

His use of the romance tradition is one in which the absolute of masculine self-centredness, with its imperative and lonely need to undergo its selfing *in extremis*, is subject to more or less successful feminine *correction* before returning to its customary bachelor solipsism. The sado-masochistic connotations of 'correction' are used deliberately. It is, of course, precisely the force of unaccommodated, brooding female sexuality in the person of Sarah in *The French Lieutenant's Woman* which could be seen as responsible for the break-up of the nineteenth-century synthesis. In this sense, the absence of a fully reciprocated adult sexual relationship through most of Fowles's work – like, for example, a comparable rarity in Dickens – should be read as an aspect of his social criticism. That artistically productive immaturity of Fowles, to which he himself refers (*MR*, 'Hardy'), can itself be seen as symptomatic, and the plots of sexual emancipation in his books are subjected to the forces of mythic recurrence, not only because he owes much to romance but because the culture as a whole is, as one reviewer of *Daniel Martin* noted of Fowles, 'always growing up'.[37] This is a syndrome with which *Daniel Martin* shows some impatience but little ability to cure. Indeed, the realistic elaboration of that book intensifies the problem.

Fowles's women tend throughout to divide between *narratological* virgins who are secret and thus mysteriously impenetrable (they may or may not be physically virgin) and whores (who may or may not be sexually experienced). This is, of course, one version of a type of division that Leslie Fiedler has noted as being native to the romance tradition as a whole. Fowles's commitment, however, has always been to a view of fiction as humanly accountable, as 'a marvellous changer of human sensibility' (*JML*, p. 183), and it is relevant here that recent narratological theory has tended to distinguish the question 'Who speaks?' from the question 'Who sees?' – a distinction sometimes lost in the Anglo-American emphasis on seeking answers only to the first question.[38] Whether or not they actually *narrate* the action, women in Fowles's second category are frequently rejected or defiled and murdered, while those in the first may still be worshipped and pursued. Miranda in *The Collector* is the first such victim of narrative penetration, seen intrinsically, pornographically stripped of her secrecy, persecuted and killed. In *The Magus* Alison's 'lostness' puts her partly outside the narrator's selfish imaginative purview, and it is the function of Lily and Conchis's manipulations to force him to begin to imagine her – an imagining necessarily projected beyond the scope of the book. In *The French Lieutenant's Woman*, male omniscience is unresisted by Tina and Mrs Poulteney (both ejected from the action) but defeated by Sarah.[39] In 'The Ebony Tower' we are invited to measure Williams's failure by his inability to replace his known wife by the mysterious Diana. In 'The Cloud' the defilement and possible murder or suicide of Catherine follows hard upon the passage in which the action is focused through her. The notorious openness of Fowles's endings, which he has presented as part of a battle against consolation, is partly consequent on the fact

93

that a closed ending would, as indeed it does in *Daniel Martin*, convert one kind of heroine into the other. And the famous forking of the narrative in *The French Lieutenant's Woman* is caused, again and crucially, not by the problematics of the legacy or the colonial emigration, which are quite as much the staple devices of Victorian narrative closure, but by the problem, once again, of the accessibility of the *princesse lointaine*.

*

This problem is three times referred to in *Daniel Martin* (pp. 428, 576, 582), but is resolved in the end with a conscious – and highly consequential – suppression of formal anxiety by her attainment, just as his desire to re-enter the childhood paradise of Thorncombe is also indulged. If, as I have argued, loss and explicability (possession) for Fowlesian heroes are linked – and Daniel Martin soliloquizes that he expects 'the loss of all his mistresses, and in more or less direct proportion to his discovery of them' (p. 256) – then this novel becomes something of a test case, which tries to face up to what could be called the narratological consequences of female emancipation by incorporating the first-person account of one of its heroines (as did *The Collector*), but in a novel where the hero is squired by a full range of familial and social obligations that become in their turn narrative responsibilities. The sinister *Frauendienst* of Clegg, which the book criticized, was easily converted into his punishment of Miranda when she refused the sanctity that his fantastic sexual chivalry wished upon her. Clegg's hypocritical self-abasement sought the correction of a good strict woman, a correction achieved by both Urfe and Smithson, and by the novels that produce them in terms of the self-consciousness of their conventionalization.

Fowles has described *Daniel Martin* as 'a very long novel about Englishness' and about his own '100 per cent selfish' generation. In this worst received of his novels, neither hero nor work seeks the usual correction, and, thus uncircumscribed, the novel returns to 'the middle-ground' of realism (ZB, p. 124), scarcely attenuated by the formal gadgetry with which it is tricked out. Once the usual deprivations are gainsaid and the hero achieves, after a twenty-year delay, his erotic quest, the novel itself surrenders to that *mange-tout* sententiousness which threatens much that Fowles has written. It is peculiar among contemporary British fiction in being a Condition-of-England novel with a partly autobiographical hero. Daniel Martin's possible writerly soubriquet is S. Wolfe, an anagram of Fowles,[40] and, though Martin is carefully distinguished from Fowles in a number of respects, he is also identified with him. Angus Wilson's *No Laughing Matter* (1967) and Margaret Drabble's *The Ice-Age* (1977) also address themselves explicitly to the possibilities and limitations of the culture, but distance the problem of authorship itself rather differently. The nearest parallel in its mixture of imbricate artifice, claustrophobic confessional and cultural prognostication is Doris Lessing's fine *The Golden Notebook* (1962), an altogether more achieved work of art. The absence of ultimate boundaries to the heroic and incontinent self-regard of the hero, whose consciousness is glorified as the high and solitary place in which we can find the best and worst of the ignoble culture he represents and defines himself against, makes for a painfully and formally self-indulgent novel. This unenclosed self-regard, indeed, is repeatedly hypostatized as a *faiblesse* of the culture it annexes, for whose bankruptcies the character of Daniel Martin requires to be read as a synecdoche.

The novel covers more than a quarter of a century of English life; it has an ambitious geographical and social range, and a largesse of historical contingency. Technically there are gestures towards cinematic effects, such as flash-forward and flashback, cut and close-up, to accord with Martin's career as filmscript writer; but the chief formal innovation is the alternating use of first and third person, sometimes within the same sentence ('I feel in his pocket and bring out a clasp-knife', p. 16) in order to evoke the hero's and the epoch's balkanized consciousness, the fragmentation of the 'unified self' into the pathos of a needy subjectivity and a reifying, third-person commentary.[41] The ease of movement between the voices tends both to create and to undercut the illusion of perspective.

It opens in an Edenic wartime Devon, a Lawrentian or Hardyesque sacred combe in which – *Et in Arcadia ego* – German and English bloodlust equally stalk. Ravens, Dan's 'totem-bird' (p. 643), alert us to the symbolic purport of landscape, pursuing Daniel through the sterile deserts of Hollywood and New Mexico as well as the fertile/sterile landscapes of lower Egypt and Syria. These are places of vocational purification, through which Martin and his sister-in-law princess must pass, along with a Castle Perilous in the form of the Krak des Chevaliers in Syria. Daniel himself is a Baudelairian dandy who lived and slept at Oxford in front of a number of mirrors. Engaged to be married there to Nell, he realizes too late that he loves and is loved by her sister Jane, with whom he enjoys and suffers the single sexual tryst of Fowlesian romance. In the intervening two decades before they come together again, a variety of women, bourgeois and proletarian, urban and bucolic, service his creative and physical requirements. The novel identifies its form with that of bourgeois melodrama (p. 611), a sentimental mode superannuated by the French Revolution, and the epigraph indeed comes from Gramsci: 'The crisis consists precisely in the fact that the old is dying and the new cannot be born; in this interregnum a great variety of morbid symptoms appear.' It also identifies its strategy implicitly with the Lukácsian view of Walter Scott, the 'cunning mediocrity' of whose heroes (p. 532) displayed the internal social dynamic of the age.

In *Daniel Martin* the inhuman generosity of the action repeatedly and punctually serves the cunning mediocrity of its hero. Nell happily leaves him for a shrewd upper-class dodo; his brother-in-law, Anthony, dying of cancer, defenestrates himself to release his widow Jane for Daniel. Dan's mistress Jenny is equally obliging. She is introduced as 'a twentieth century princess, provoking very nearly the same dream as the real princesses who once languished in their walled castles and haunted another age besotted with the concept of the unattainable' (p. 70). She is a young and beautiful film star whom he admonishes not to fall in love with him (p. 48), since romantic love is a selfish sickness of his own still-Victorian generation. His narrative is intermitted with hers, and, when it has become apparent that she does indeed love him, she sends him an unhappy account of a sexual infidelity, real or imagined. Since it arrives at exactly the point when he and Jane are moving together again, it provides him with an excellent pretext for rejecting her, which he does not long neglect. The rejection is accompanied by a sermon in which he advises her that as a beautiful and successful actress she will be regarded by her public as a sacrosanct 'vestal *virgin*' (for vestal virgins, it will be remembered, loss of virginity was punishable by death), while she already inhabits a social world 'where the stock model for every relationship is really that between a ponce and *whore*' (p. 660; my italics).

Dan is left with Jane, a less compromised madonna with 'authenticity-obsessed eyes', another secret existentialist heroine whose Catholicism and Marxism are neither of them directly perceived. Indeed, once more, and unlike the hapless Jenny, the action is again never focused through her, and it is part of her value to remain safely inexplicable: 'She was not the sort of woman ever to be understood empirically, logically' (p. 321). The language varies bewilderingly from the high specific-ity of the first chapter – in which 'swaling', 'haulm', 'bartons, leats and linhays' and 'marly' are used with a precise attentive-ness – to the tired and unfastidious locutions of much of the rest of the book, in which a silence is 'like a scream' (p. 143), a marriage has 'hidden cancer' (p. 153), the hero sleeps a 'slum-ber . . . of the damned' (p. 113), and an 'iron curtain' (p. 204) separates people. As Lever shows, there are a dozen instances of characters biting their lips in a half-smile. Above all, how-ever, the novel is characterized by a language in which the organicist life-force of the moral agent is once more perceived as risking neutering and death. This language of romantic excess and romantic paranoia gives us Martin 'paralysed, stunned by the enormity, ravished by the strangeness' (p. 67), Anthony 'embalmed' by his house, censorship 'castrating' the theatre (p. 171), Jenny 'crucified' by her own good looks (p.

70), and Martin himself 'excluded, castrated by both capitalism and socialism, forbidden to belong' (p. 611) and 'dwarfed' in his century (p. 667). The hyperbolic language of victimization occurs in every Fowles work; and 'castration' and 'extermination', in particular, are favourite Fowlesian tropes. William Blake, too, is normally quoted as though he were an apostle only of romantic liberation. What is distinct in *Daniel Martin* is the injection of these elements into a fiction so much more quixotically obligated towards realism than anything else he has attempted. In the earlier romances they naturalize less uncomfortably. Here Fowles's natural allegiance towards a more romantic version of realism, with its division of the world between idealism and determinism, quarrels unwittingly with a form committed to finding an overview from which to transcend such discontinuities. The author-hero, '*caged* . . . like an inefficient *god*' (p. 247), '*imprisoned*' in his gifts (p. 295; my italics), a wounded Saviour, mirrors a vision of the moral agent both as omnipotent monarch and impotent puppet, which we often find in romance. If Fowles has until now sometimes been more interesting as a writer than he is good, it may be a consequence of the ways his vision flatters our presuppositions as well as his. *Daniel Martin* does read as a falling-off; but it is too early to tell to what degree Fowles's partial disengagement in his long struggle with the problematics of his chosen form marks a new epoch in his writing.

In her introduction to *The Golden Notebook* (1962), Doris Lessing movingly describes that contemporary artistic impasse where the writer, trying to transcend 'the driving painful individuality of the art of the bourgeois era', finds it difficult to avoid being 'intensely subjective', hard to find ways of making the personal general. In modern anxiety one fundamental archetype, the 'monstrously isolated, monstrously narcissistic, pedestalled paragon', the artist, confronts another, his 'mirror image the businessman' – one shown as the boorish insensitive, the other as the creator, but each requiring to be shriven because of what they produce (*NT*, p. 174). The two decades since that introduction, during which Fowles published and became known, have seen the adoption by many new writers of various experimental attempts to deploy a new type of artistic impersonality and engage with a less romantic and hubristic version of their task. The period has seen an increasing democratization and demoticization of the arts, and also the continued siphoning off of a small mandarin audience for what once used to be called the 'art novel'. Serious fiction has felt its own displacement; Fowles, though, has declared the intention to reach all constituencies, and mediate, in his chosen terms, between the Few and the Many. It is an accommodation which, for all its worthy messages of comfort, has not been attempted without a certain cost.

Fowles's particular anxious vision of the writer as Solitary Citizen of the city-state of Art, facing and ameliorating an unregenerate majority – together with his shifty concern with sexual depuritanization – makes him sometimes look like our last and not our least glib Edwardian: his audience, like his heroes, can be so placed that there is greater investment in their pleasurable punishment than in their reform. If his claims for his work have not always been granted the seriousness he would wish, this may have to do with their often present note of unremarkable compromise, producing uncertainties of control and an unsustained intellectual ambitiousness. The free figure of Robin Hood – the man washed free, like good art, of the sin of existing – has been resonant to Fowles personally; it has also been used as an image of refusal at its most equivocal, to 'project the bourgeois's own slight margin of resentment against the safe commercial way of life he has desired'.[42] That margin of historical resentment has always been strong for Fowles, but hard to negotiate. None the less it displays his taste for the unconditioned, to which all his astonishingly various fictions ingeniously cater, and which is surely the one democratic prejudice we all share.

APPENDIX: THE FILM OF
'THE FRENCH LIEUTENANT'S WOMAN'

A possibly apocryphal story has it that Woody Allen, asked how he would live his life again if reincarnated, answered that he would avoid seeing the film of *The Magus*. The film of *The Collector* was undistinguished, that of *The Magus* worse, but that made from *The French Lieutenant's Woman* was from the start a different proposition. The script was written by Harold Pinter, who, besides being a playwright of great distinction, is also a writer of screenplays of notable brilliance and economy.

The film tackles the problem of finding analogues in cinematic terms for the self-relexiveness, multiple endings, and all-pervasive tonal play of the narrative voice of the novel, with characteristic nerve and originality. The solution, apparently suggested by the director Karel Reisz, was to set the love-story of Charles and Sarah within another, the location romance of the actors presented as portraying them. The modern love-affair then acts as an acoustic chamber within which the Victorian affair can resonate, amplifying and ironizing some of its meanings. It is a brilliant device. Among the sacrifices made to it are Charles's uncle, Mrs Poulteney's demise, the prostitute pseudo-Sarah, and, inevitably, the epistemological drama acted out by the discursive play, in the novel, of the authorial commentary. Some of the historical documentation is carried out by the modern lovers who, for example, discuss the statistics of Victorian prostitution; a version of the imbrication of narrative levels is retained as we seem invited impertinently to ponder what can be the relations between the actors Jeremy Irons and Meryl Streep, who portray the actors Mike and Anna, who purportedly play the roles of Charles and Sarah; and a sense of the interpenetration of fiction and history, another of the novel's distinctive signatures, also precariously survives. Above all, the device permits a stunning and ingenious solution to the problem of the endings, as each story-line pursues, separately but with increasing convergence, its own crisis.

The action of Pinter's imagination on Fowles's, however, has some odd effects. Necessary compression and elision in a Pinter screenplay – *The Servant*, for example – often distils an aesthetic pleasure quite as powerful, or more so, than the book afforded. Pinter is a master of reticence, Fowles an apprentice, and in the case of the film of *The French Lieutenant's Woman* there is a certain blandness, the echoes ringing somewhat hollowly on occasion. If it is not Pinter's best screenplay, it is none the less a remarkable commentary on the novel.[43]

POSTSCRIPT: 'MANTISSA'

Mantissa is a slight but a stock-taking novel, and its inhospitable reception invites the critic, too, to take stock. *Mantissa* is *about* the quarrel with his female muse which I have been suggesting has formed the secret plot of all Fowles's fiction. My argument has been that all Fowles's books in effect share such a secret plot. In *Mantissa* this hidden plot comes out into the open.

Fowles's romances take their force from an Oedipal conflict between sexual desire and fear. In 'Hardy' Fowles adverts to this and strongly endorses a Freudian reading of *The French Lieutenant's Woman*, in which we recall that Sarah makes her appearance on the last page as a sphinx. It was Oedipus alone who was able to decipher the sphinx's riddle, so killing her, and Fowles's novels have long been prone to imagining their female agents, in a classically Oedipal formation, as either innocent or guilty. An ostentatiously liberal sexual politics repeatedly negotiates the force of play of a coercive and repressive sexual fantasy. Much of the formal play of the books is generated to serve or disguise this. *Mantissa* openly concerns the writer's struggles with his muse, a physical and emotional and intellectual struggle which is decked out or embarrassed, according to your point of view, by much intellectually ambitious allusion to classical and other sources.

Fowles, I have argued, has always had some special claim to the topic of sexual depuritanization. For the hero of *Daniel*

Martin two aspects of censorship, 'masturbation and blasphemy' (*DM*, p. 91) were inextricably linked, and his contemporaries were 'all brought up to some degree in the nineteenth century' since 'the twentieth century did not begin until 1945' (*DM*, p. 94). In *The Magus* Nicholas Urfe's parents 'never rose sufficiently above history to leave . . . the grotesquely elongated shadow . . . of that monstrous dwarf Queen Victoria' (*M*, p. 15) so that Urfe has to attempt the appropriate historical levitation himself. Fowles's books are pious in particular about the emancipation of their female agents, whom the action tends to victimize. Perhaps Fowles's popularity in the 1960s, when the enfranchisement of the libido was held to be so strict an existential duty, owed something to this mixture. He has also noted the complicity of fiction itself in repression, as the pleasures of the text depend on a delayed gratification in a contest between secrecy and revelation. 'The characteristic abundance of the Victorian novel . . . can be partly attributed to the taboo on sexual frankness' ('Hardy' p. 42).

Exactly such a contest feeds all his work, and accounts both for the erotic casuistry he achieves at his best, and also the high-minded and facetious prurience to which his writing at its worst descends. *All* fiction, in some sense, must turn sex into discourse, but Fowles's Romantic Eros can on occasion be the vehicle of a skittish and humourless titillation. It seems to me no accident that Fowles's heroines so often partake of the ambience of the Pre-Raphaelite Brotherhood. The PRB act out the necessary and fantastic blend of wistful medievalism and militant 'modernity' that best enshrines that blend of femininity Fowles likes to imagine. In one story after another the feudalizing and modernizing of relations between the sexes are shown to be linked, and the liaison between two kinds of fantasy – 'liberation' and 'courtly love' – is perpetually resolemnized.

The process by which sex translates itself into discourse becomes the subject matter and the plot of *Mantissa*. Like the earlier novels *Mantissa* takes place in a small enclosure and makes much play with it. Miles Green regains consciousness in what seems to be a private room in a hospital. The room is

103

covered in quilting of a uniform pale grey and the floor is flesh pink. Green has lost his memory and no longer knows who he is. His wife fails to trigger any recall of his past life and once she has left him, the desirable Dr Delphie and her assistant – the equally desirable black nurse Cory – set to work on his libido. Explaining that memory is linked to sexual activity they vie with one another in attempting to rouse Miles sexually. Miles's amnesia is equalled by a certain coy prudishness. At the end of this first part (there are four), Miles is delivered of a manuscript. The room here, recalling the crypt of *The Collector* or the asylum in which Dr Grogan had tempted Charles to have Sarah incarcerated in *The French Lieutenant's Woman*, is at last what all such enclosures had distantly proposed themselves to be: it is the inside of Miles's head. The decoration recalls the brain.

In the following three parts this male brain becomes the seat of that psychomachia I suggested all Fowles's work is involved in: the quarrel between the female soul or *anima* which is outside history, and the male intelligence which wishes to celebrate and exploit her, to be inspired and punished by her. Here Dr Delphie moves between contemporary doctor, punk rock star with an electric guitar, be-tunicked Goddess with a lyre and vaudeville artiste. She is Erato, muse of lyric poetry. As for Mantissa itself, a footnote late in the novel teasingly reminds us that it is 'an addition of comparatively small importance, especially to a literary effort or discourse' (p. 185); it is also, perhaps, that other addition of debatable importance, the male sexual parts. Fowles struggles with his muse as Miles Green wrestles and argues with this changeable girl, in an action which confuses the attempt at each stage to decide whether or not it is 'literal' or 'metaphoric'.

For this critic *Mantissa* brings to the fore two deep and potentially damaging reservations about his work. It is everywhere apparent that Fowles wishes to be a European, which is to say an intellectual, novelist. The novels however, show him to be more showman or journalist-of-ideas than intellectual. Moreover, it is possible to be a great writer without submitting any such credentials. Consider Dickens, in no conceivable sense an intellectual writer for all his intelligence, yet incontrovertibly great.

The example of Dickens brings home my second reservation. 'The novel is a comic form. A novel which isn't at all comic is in great danger, aesthetically speaking' (*ZB*, p. 230), one of Fowles's contemporaries has pointed out. The novel is the most genially accommodating and imperfect of all the great art forms. To recall the examples of Dickens or of Hardy is to realize that it can survive vulgarity, pretension, self-regard and almost any sin you care to mention. What it cannot survive is want of humour. Even Kafka and Dostoevsky are deeply, darkly comic. To say that *Mantissa* is an unfunny book, and Fowles a quite astonishingly unfunny writer, is to say a great deal about what limits his achievement, and about how damaging this disability is. That he remains none the less oddly undismissable is a paradoxical tribute to the gifts he undoubtedly possesses; and not the least of these is his narrative power.

NOTES

1 For discussions of romance, see Ronald Binns, 'John Fowles: Radical Romancer', *Critical Quarterly*, 15 (Winter 1973), pp. 317–34; Gillian Beer, *The Romance* (London and New York, 1970); Leslie Fiedler, *Love and Death in the American Novel* (London and New York, 1967); Northrop Frye, *Anatomy of Criticism* (Princeton, NJ, 1957).

2 For accounts of Fowles's critical reception, see Barry and Toni Olshen, *John Fowles: A Reference Guide* (Boston, Mass., 1980).

3 Robert Scholes, *Fabulation and Meta-Fiction* (Urbana and Chicago, Ill., and London, 1979), p. 37.

4 In J. Harari (ed.), *Textual Strategies: Perspectives in Post-Structuralist Criticism* (London and New York, 1979), p. 124.

5 Henry James, *The Art of the Novel* (London and New York, 1934), p. 33.

6 Ronald Binns, op. cit., p. 319.

7 W. H. Auden, *The Enchafed Flood, or The Romantic Iconography of the Sea* (London, 1951), p. 125.

8 Angus Wilson, *The Wild Garden* (Berkeley, Calif., 1965), p. 146.

9 Catherine Belsey, *Critical Practice* (London and New York, 1980).

10 In J. Wakerman (ed.), *World Authors 1950–1970* (New York, 1975), p. 485.

11 Auden, op. cit., p. 30.

12 For another account of *The Aristos*, see *JML*, pp. 163–80.

13 For a different account of Fowles's existentialism, see Robert Scholes, *Structuralism in Literature* (New Haven, Conn., and London, 1974), which sees Fowles as moving from existentialism towards structuralism.

14 E. P. Thompson, *The Poverty of Theory* (London, 1978), p. 31.

15 Thus Fowles has also shown a tenderness towards such little-known writers as Richard Jefferies, Claire de Durfort, S. Baring-Gould (see Bibliography).

16 Iris Murdoch, 'Existentialists and Mystics', in W. H. Robson (ed.), *Essays and Poems Presented to Lord David Cecil* (London, 1970), p. 172.

17 Iris Murdoch, *The Sovereignty of Good* (London, 1970), p. 48.

18 Frank Kermode, *The Sense of an Ending* (London and New York, 1966), p. 138.

19 See Iris Murdoch, 'Existentialists and Mystics' and *The Sovereignty of Good*, pp. 48–50. For Murdoch's views on the ills of Romanticism, see also 'Against Dryness: A Polemical Sketch', *Encounter*, 16 (January 1961), pp. 16–20, collected in Malcolm Bradbury (ed.), *The Novel Today* (London, 1977); see also 'The Sublime and the Beautiful Revisited', *The Yale Review*, 49 (1959), pp. 247–71.

20 I owe this point to Olshen.

21 Again, I owe this point to Olshen.

22 Scholes, op. cit., 1979, p. 39.

23 Nicholas Brooke, 'Shakespeare and the Baroque', *British Academy Proceedings*, 63 (1978).

24 For full accounts of Fowles's revisions, see *JML*, pp. 236–46; and Ronald Binns, 'A New Version of *The Magus*', *Critical Quarterly*, 19 (Winter 1977), pp. 79–84.

25 Gillian Beer, op. cit., p. 8.

26 Virginia Woolf, *Moments of Being* (London, 1978), p. 84.

27 The phrase is Lorna Sage's in *New Review*, 1, 6 (1974–5), p. 41.

28 For a Freudian reading of *FLW*, which Fowles has endorsed, see Gilbert J. Rose, '*The French Lieutenant's Woman*: The Unconscious Significance of a Novel to its Author', *American Imago*, 29 (Summer 1972), pp. 165–76.

29 See Barbara Hardy, Introduction to *Daniel Deronda* (Harmondsworth, 1976).

30 Fowles endorses this view in 'Hardy and the Hag'. For earlier drafts of *FLW* which throw much light on the problems Fowles experienced with the endings, see *JML*, pp. 275–86. In one draft his creator dresses up as an escaped maniac and threatens Charles with an axe.

31 For Fowles's ambivalence about sexual depuritanization, see, importantly, 'Hardy': 'the characteristic abundance of the Victorian novel . . . can be partly attributed to the taboo on sexual frankness'. See also *FLW*, ch. 35, which partly subscribes to the theory that 'progress' springs from repression; and *A*, p. 174. As both Brantlinger and Lever have differently argued, Fowles is in a sense the last Edwardian.

32 Henry James, *The House of Fiction* (London, 1962), p. 101.

33 A point made by John Mills, 'Fowles's Indeterminacy: An Art of

Alternatives', *West Coast Review*, 10 (October 1975), pp. 32–6.

34 Constance Hieatt, '*Eliduc* Revisited: John Fowles and Marie de France', *English Studies in Canada*, 3 (Fall 1977), p. 357.

35 See C. S. Lewis, *The Allegory of Love* (London, 1936), *passim*.

36 J. S. Mill, *On the Subjection of Women* (1869), p. 258.

37 Lorna Sage, 'Grave New World', *Observer*, 9 October 1977, p. 27.

38 See Gérard Genette, *Narrative Discourse* (Ithaca, NY, and Oxford, 1980), esp. chapters 4 and 5.

39 A point driven home by the book's final reference to Sarah, as advantageously 'fitting the role of the sphinx' (*FLW*, p. 399): once Oedipus had solved the riddle of the sphinx, she destroyed herself. Like the sphinx, Sarah's survival depends on her 'impenetrability'.
   Sarah's 'modernity' at the end, it should be noted, is a characteristically ambiguous commodity. By being recruited to the ambience of the Pre-Raphaelite Brotherhood she can, like Diana in *ET*, suggest a 'modern' sexuality which is none the less safely and wistfully medievalized and belongs to courtly romance.

40 A point made by David Walker, 'Subversion of Narrative in the Work of André Gide and John Fowles', *Comparative Criticism: A Yearbook*, vol. 2 (Cambridge, 1980), pp. 187–212.

41 For a different account of this feature, see Simon Loveday, 'The Style of John Fowles: Tense and Person in the First Chapter of *Daniel Martin*', *The Journal of Narrative Technique*, 10, 3 (Fall 1980), pp. 198–204.

42 Fiedler, op. cit., p. 165. Daniel Martin wrote a film script about Robin Hood too.

43 For further discussion of these points, see Peter J. Conradi, '*The French Lieutenant's Woman*: Novel: Screenplay: Film', *Critical Quarterly*, 24, 1 (Spring 1982).

BIBLIOGRAPHY

WORKS BY JOHN FOWLES

Fiction

The Collector. London: Cape, 1963. Boston, Mass.: Little, Brown, 1963.
The Magus. Boston, Mass.: Little, Brown, 1965. London: Cape, 1966.
The French Lieutenant's Woman. London: Cape, 1969. Boston, Mass.: Little, Brown, 1969.
The Ebony Tower. London: Cape, 1974. Boston, Mass.: Little, Brown, 1974.
Daniel Martin. London: Cape, 1977. Boston, Mass.: Little, Brown, 1977.
The Magus: A Revised Version. London: Cape, 1977. Boston, Mass.: Little, Brown, 1978.
Mantissa. London: Cape, 1982. Boston, Mass.: Little, Brown, 1982.

Non-fiction

Afterword to Henri Alain-Fournier, *The Wanderer (Le Grand Meaulnes)*. New York: New American Library, 1971.
The Aristos: A Self-Portrait in Ideas. Boston, Mass.: Little, Brown, 1964. London: Cape, 1965.
The Enigma of Stonehenge (with Barry Brukoff). London: Cape, 1980.
Foreword and Afterword to Sir Arthur Conan Doyle, *The Hound of the Baskervilles*. London: Murray and Cape, 1974.
Foreword to *The Lais of Marie de France*. New York: E. P. Dutton, 1978.
Foreword to the screenplay of *The French Lieutenant's Woman*. London: Cape, 1981. Boston, Mass.: Little, Brown, 1981.
'Hardy and the Hag'. In L. St John Butler (ed.), *Thomas Hardy after Fifty Years*, pp. 28–42. London: Macmillan, 1977.
Introduction to Richard Jefferies, *After London or Wild England*. London: Oxford University Press, 1980.

Introduction, Glossary and Appendix to S. Baring-Gould, *Mehalah: A Story of the Salt Marshes*. London: Chatto & Windus, 1969.

'Is the Novel Dead?' *Books*, 1 (Autumn 1970), pp. 2–5.

Islands (with Fay Godwin). London: Cape, 1978. Boston, Mass.: Little, Brown, 1978.

'I Write Therefore I Am'. *Evergreen Review*, 8 (August–September 1964), pp. 16–17, 89–90.

'*The Magus* Revisited'. *The Times*, 28 May 1977, p. 7. Reprinted as 'Why I Rewrote *The Magus*', *Saturday Review*, 18 February 1978, pp. 25–30.

'My Recollections of Kafka'. *Mosaic*, 3 (Summer 1970), pp. 31–41. Reprinted in R. G. Collins and K. McRobbie (eds), *New Views of Franz Kafka*. Winnipeg: University of Manitoba Press, 1974.

'Notes on Writing a Novel'. *Harper's Magazine* (July 1968). Reprinted under various titles in *The Cornhill Magazine* (Summer 1969) (an edited version); in Malcolm Bradbury (ed.), *The Novel Today* (Manchester and London: Manchester University Press and Fontana, 1977); and T. McCormack (ed.), *Afterwards: Novelists on their Novels* (New York: Harper & Row, 1969).

'On Being English But Not British'. *The Texas Quarterly*, 7 (Autumn 1964), pp. 154–62.

Poems. New York and Toronto: Ecco Press, 1973.

'Seeing Nature Whole'. *Harper's Magazine*, 259 (November 1979), pp. 49–68.

Shipwreck. London: Cape, 1974. Boston, Mass.: Little, Brown, 1975.

Steepholm: A Case History in the Study of Evolution (with R. Legg). London: Kenneth Allsop Memorial Trust, 1978.

Translation of Charles Perrault, *Cinderella*. London: Cape, 1974. Boston, Mass.: Little, Brown, 1976.

Translation of Claire de Durfort, *Ourika*. Austin, Tex.: W. Thomas Taylor, 1977.

The Tree. London: Aurum Press, 1979. Boston, Mass.: Little, Brown, 1980.

SELECTED CRITICISM OF JOHN FOWLES

Books

Huffaker, Robert. *John Fowles*. Boston, Mass.: G. K. Hall, 1980. (Contains an annotated bibliography.)

Olshen, Barry. *John Fowles*. New York: Ungar, 1978.

Olshen, Barry and Toni. *John Fowles: A Reference Guide*. Boston, Mass.: G. K. Hall, 1980. (Contains abstracts of major articles and books up to 1979.)

Palmer, W. J. *The Fiction of John Fowles: Tradition, Art, and the Loneliness of Selfhood.* Columbia, Mo.: University of Missouri Press, 1974.

Wolfe, Peter. *John Fowles, Magus and Moralist.* Lewisburg, Pa: Bucknell University Press, 1976. London: Associated University Press, 1976.

Selected articles

Binns, Ronald. 'John Fowles: Radical Romancer'. *Critical Quarterly*, 15 (Winter 1973), pp. 317–34.

——'A New Version of *The Magus*'. *Critical Quarterly*, 19 (Winter 1977), pp. 79–84.

Boston, Richard. 'John Fowles, Alone But Not Lonely'. *New York Times Book Review*, 9 November 1969, pp. 2, 52–3.

Bradbury, Malcolm. 'John Fowles' *The Magus*'. In Brom Weber (ed.), *Sense and Sensibility in Twentieth Century Writing*, pp. 26–38. Carbondale, Ill.: Southern Illinois University Press, 1970. Reprinted with changes as 'The Novelist as Impresario: John Fowles and his Magus'. In *Possibilities: Essays on the State of the Novel*, pp. 256–71. London: Oxford University Press, 1973.

Brantlinger, Patrick, Adam, Ian, and Rothblatt, Sheldon. '*The French Lieutenant's Woman*: A Discussion'. *Victorian Studies*, 15 (March 1972), pp. 339–56.

Burden, Robert. 'The Novel Interrogates Itself: Parody as Self-Consciousness in Contemporary English Fiction'. In M. Bradbury and D. Palmer (eds), *The Contemporary English Novel*, pp. 133–55. Stratford-upon-Avon Studies, 18. London: Edward Arnold, 1979.

Campbell, James. 'An Interview with John Fowles'. *Contemporary Literature*, 17, 4 (1976), pp. 455–69.

Conradi, Peter J. '*The French Lieutenant's Woman*: Novel: Screenplay: Film'. *Critical Quarterly*, 24 (Spring 1982).

De Vitis, A. A., and Palmer, William J. '*A Pair of Blue Eyes* Flash at *The French Lieutenant's Woman*'. *Contemporary Literature*, 15 (Winter 1974), pp. 90–101.

Eddins, Dwight. 'John Fowles: Existence as Authorship'. *Contemporary Literature*, 17 (Spring 1976), pp. 204–22.

Evarts, Prescott, Jr. 'Fowles' *The French Lieutenant's Woman* as Tragedy'. *Critique*, 13 (1972), pp. 57–69.

Halpern, Daniel. 'A Sort of Exile in Lyme Regis'. *London Magazine*, 10 (March 1971), pp. 34–46.

Hieatt, Constance. '*Eliduc* Revisited: John Fowles and Marie de France'. *English Studies in Canada*, 3 (Fall 1977), pp. 351–8.

Journal of Modern Literature, 8, 2 (1980–1). John Fowles Special Number. (Contains a dozen articles on the full range of Fowles's work.)

Kaplan, Fred. 'Victorian Modernists: Fowles and Nabokov'. *The Journal of Narrative Technique*, 3 (May 1973), pp. 108–20.

Lever, Karen. 'The Education of John Fowles'. *Critique*, 21 (1979), pp. 85–99.

Lodge, David. 'Ambiguously Ever After: Problematical Endings in English Fiction'. In *Working with Structuralism*. London and Boston, Mass.: Routledge & Kegan Paul, 1981.

Loveday, Simon. 'The Style of John Fowles: Tense and Person in the First Chapter of *Daniel Martin*'. *The Journal of Narrative Technique*, 10, 3 (Fall 1980), pp. 198–204.

Mills, John. 'Fowles' Indeterminacy: An Art of Alternatives'. *West Coast Review*, 10 (October 1975), pp. 32–6.

Newquist, Roy (ed.). 'John Fowles'. In *Counterpoint*, pp. 217–25. Chicago, Ill.: Rand McNally, 1964.

Rankin, Elizabeth D. 'Cryptic Coloration in *The French Lieutenant's Woman*'. *The Journal of Narrative Technique*, 3 (September 1973), pp. 193–207.

Ricks, Christopher. 'The Unignorable Real'. *New York Review of Books*, 12 February 1970, pp. 22–4.

Robinson, Robert. 'Giving the Reader a Choice – a Conversation with John Fowles'. *The Listener*, 31 October 1974, p. 584.

Rose, Gilbert J. '*The French Lieutenant's Woman*: The Unconscious Significance of a Novel to its Author'. *American Imago*, 29 (Summer 1972), pp. 165–76.

Rothblatt, *see* Brantlinger.

Sage, Lorna. 'John Fowles'. *The New Review*, 1 (October 1974), pp. 31–7.

Scholes, Robert. 'The Illiberal Imagination'. *New Literary History*, 4 (Spring 1973), pp. 521–40. Partly reprinted in *Structuralism in Literature*, ch. 6. New Haven, Conn., and London: Yale University Press, 1974.

——'The Orgastic Fiction of John Fowles'. *The Hollins Critics*, 6 (December 1969), pp. 1–12. Reprinted in *Fabulation and Metafiction*. Urbana and Chicago, Ill., and London: University of Illinois Press, 1979.

Stolley, Richard. 'The French Lieutenant's Woman's Man'. *Life*, 29 May 1970, pp. 55–60.

Walker, David. 'Subversion of Narrative in the work of André Gide and John Fowles'. *Comparative Criticism: A Yearbook*, vol. 2 (Cambridge, 1980), pp. 187–212.